· T R O P H I E S ·

Teacher's Edition
Practice Book

Grade 2 ◆ Volume Two

Harcourt

Orlando   Boston   Dallas   Chicago   San Diego

Visit *The Learning Site!*
www.harcourtschool.com

Contents

BANNER DAYS

► **Write the words where they belong in the chart.**

how	crown	out	brow	around
mouth	now	house	found	clown

c<u>ow</u>

m<u>ou</u>se

how	out
crown	around
brow	mouth
now	house
clown	found

SCHOOL-HOME CONNECTION Work with your child to think of a sentence using both an *ou* word and an *ow* word, such as *There's a clown in my house.*

1

Practice Book
Banner Days

Name _____

▶ **Read the Spelling Words. Sort the words and write them where they belong.**

Spelling Words

Words with *ou*	
1. _____ found	6. _____ around
2. _____ house	7. _____ without
3. _____ mouth	**Words with *ow***
4. _____ out	8. _____ brow
5. _____ sound	9. _____ how
	10. _____ now

how
mouth
out
house
without
found
around
sound
now
brow
beauties
skies
started
mean
cow

▶ **Sort the words that are left by the number of syllables.**

One-Syllable Words	Two-Syllable Words
11. _____ skies	14. _____ beauties
12. _____ mean	15. _____ started
13. _____ cow	

Practice Book
Banner Days

Name _____

▶ **Solve the riddles. Write a word from the box on each line.**

round	house	mouth	crown	frown
clowns	without	cow	brow	sound

1. People live in this. It's a _____house_____.

2. This animal says "moo." It's a _____cow_____.

3. This is not with. It's _____without_____.

4. A king wears this on his head.

It's a _____crown_____.

5. This is not a smile.

It's a _____frown_____.

6. When you hear something, you hear this.

It's a _____sound_____.

7. This is the shape of a circle. It's _____round_____.

8. You talk with this. It's your _____mouth_____.

9. These funny people are in a circus.

They are _____clowns_____.

SCHOOL-HOME CONNECTION Ask your child
to draw and label a picture for one of the words
used on this page. Then ask him or her to point
out the letters that stand for the vowel sound.

Practice Book
Banner Days

▶ **Finish the story. On each line, write a word from the shirts.**

boring   ducked   sense   suppose   tractor

I ____suppose____ Grandpa lives in the best place in the

world. It's never ____boring____ on his farm. It's fun to ride on

grandpa's ____tractor____. One cold day I ____ducked____

under the barnyard fence and saw all the animals sleeping together.

I guess it made ____sense____ for the animals to sleep together to

keep warm.

 TRY THIS! Write a story about your favorite farm animal. Use as many Vocabulary Words as you can.

© Harcourt

4

Skill Reminder • **A pronoun takes the place of a noun. *I, you, he, she, it,* and *they* are pronouns.**

▶ Finish each sentence. Write a pronoun from the box that can take the place of the noun in ( ). Remember to begin each sentence with a capital letter.

I	you	he	she	they	it

1. _____He_____ went to the farm. **(Max)**

2. _____She_____ went, too. **(Liz)**

3. _____They_____ saw many farm animals. **(the children)**

4. _____They_____ were in the barn. **(the horses)**

5. _____He_____ asked about the snake. **(Mr. Jung)**

6. _____It_____ did not live on the farm. **(the snake)**

7. Mrs. Grant said, "_____I_____ liked that snake." **(Mrs. Grant)**

8. Mrs. Grant told Angie, "_____You_____ would have liked it, too." **(Angie)**

TRY THIS! Draw a picture of something you and your friends like to do. Write two sentences to go with your picture. Use the pronouns *I* and *we* in your sentences.

Name _____

| **Syllable Rule** | • **When a two-syllable word has an ending, it is usually divided between the base word and the ending. Example: fear/less wish/ful** |

▶ **On the line write the boldfaced word in syllables.**
Remember not to divide one-syllable words.

1. Rocky has _____cheer/ful_____ days.

   cheerful

2. He barks _____loud/er_____ when the doorbell rings.

   louder

3. He _____played_____ catch with me yesterday.

   played

4. Rocky _____glad/ly_____ takes long walks with me.

   gladly

5. He never _____eats_____ my shoes.

   eats

6. Rocky is _____care/ful_____ when he plays.

   careful

© Harcourt

Practice Book
Banner Days

Name _____

▶ **Read the story. Then complete the sentences.**

The Rainy Day

It was a rainy day at school. We could not play outside. The playground was soaked. After lunch, we walked back to the classroom. There we saw markers, paints, and crayons on our desks. Our teacher smiled. It was time for arts and crafts. Everyone was excited.

1. The children could not play outside because

_____
it was a rainy day

_____.

> 💡 **Tip**
>
> A cause is why something happened.

2. Everyone was excited because

_____
it was time for

_____.
arts and crafts

> 💡 **Tip**
>
> An effect can often be found just before the cause.

© Harcourt

SCHOOL-HOME CONNECTION With your child, read a newspaper article. Help your child figure out a cause and an effect of the event described.

7

Practice Book
Banner Days

Name _____

▶ **Read the story. On each line below, write the underlined word and add the correct suffix.**

Everyone was happy. It was a **(1)** joy day. It was sunny. The skies were blue and **(2)** cloud. The second grade was planting a garden. "Pay attention," said their teacher, Mrs. Dell. "Be **(3)** care." The children each buried a **(4)** hand of carrot seeds in the dirt. They had lots of carrots to use in carrot cake and carrot soup and carrot salad. One day a **(5)** sound visitor stole into their garden. It was a rabbit. The children watched the rabbit eat a **(6)** mouth of carrots.

1. _____joyful_____   2. _____cloudless_____

3. _____careful_____   4. _____handful_____

5. _____soundless_____   6. _____mouthful_____

SCHOOL-HOME CONNECTION With your child, make up sentences with words that end with –ful or –less, such as truthful, careful, nameless or timeless. Talk about the base words: truth, care, name, time. Ask your child how the ending –ful or –less changes the meaning of the base word.

Practice Book
Banner Days

© Harcourt

▶ **Circle the best answer to each riddle.**

1. This is not rough.　　　soap　(smooth)　smock　smile

2. You sweep with this.　　broad　broke　(broom)　born

3. They grow under trees.　(roots)　rope　road　role

4. This shines in the
   night sky.　　　　　　(moon)　mom　mode　mouse

5. You eat this.　　　　　fool　foam　foot　(food)

6. This is a kind of
   TV show.　　　　　　car　tune　(cartoon)　croon

7. This has two wheels,
   and you stand on it.　spring　sight　(scooter)　school

8. This is the top part
   of a house.　　　　　read　rule　rope　(roof)

9. This is like a shoe.　　(boot)　baby　book　box

10. You eat soup with this.　spool　sport　spot　(spoon)

SCHOOL-HOME CONNECTION With your child,
look around the house and write down all the
words containing *oo* for things you find.

9

Practice Book
Banner Days

© Harcourt

Name _____

▶ **Finish the story. On each line, write a word from the box.**

coin	boy	toy	cowboys
soil	point	join	

A Day to Enjoy

One day a **(1)** _____ boy _____ named

Jack was digging in the **(2)** _____ soil _____.

He found a shiny **(3)** _____ coin _____.
Jack knew what he wanted to do. "Mom, may we go

to the **(4)** _____ toy _____ store?" he asked. "Yes,
Jack," said Mom. "Let's ask your dad to

(5) _____ join _____ us." At the store, Jack found
what he was looking for. It was on a high shelf. He had to

(6) _____ point _____ to what he wanted. The clerk

took it down. She put the two **(7)** _____ cowboys _____
and two horses in Jack's hands. What a lucky day it had been
for Jack!

SCHOOL-HOME CONNECTION Show your child several different coins. Have your child name the coins and then think of other words that have the *oi* sound.

10

Practice Book
Banner Days

© Harcourt

▶ **Read the Spelling Words. Sort the words and write them where they belong.**

Spelling Words

Words with *oi*	Words with *oy*
1. coin	7. joy
2. join	8. toy
3. oil	9. cowboys
4. point	10. enjoyment
5. soil	
6. voices	

voices
cowboys
toy
enjoyment
oil
point
join
soil
joy
coin
around
without
fire
train
wait

▶ **Write the words that are left in alphabetical order.**

11. around	14. wait
12. fire	15. without
13. train	

Practice Book
Banner Days

Name _____

▶ **Solve the riddles. Write a word from the box on each line.**

spoil	voices	oil	joy	foil
toy	cowboys	soil	point	join

1. You can grow flowers in this. It's _____ soil _____.

2. A pencil has one of these. It's a _____ point _____.

3. People feel this when they are happy.

   It's _____ joy _____.

4. This may happen if you leave milk out.

   It may _____ spoil _____.

5. You do this to be part of a team.

   You _____ join _____.

6. You may use this when you cook.

   It is _____ oil _____.

7. When we sing, we use these.

   We use our _____ voices _____.

8. People wrap food in this. It's _____ foil _____.

9. A doll is one of these. It's a _____ toy _____.

10. You may find these men riding horses.

    They are _____ cowboys _____.

SCHOOL-HOME CONNECTION Ask your child
to make up riddles for the words *boy* and *boil*.
Have your child write the words and point to the
letters that make the *oi* sound.

Practice Book
Banner Days

© Harcourt

▶ **Solve the riddles. On each line, write a word from the box.**

captured	imagination	manners	matador
plains	relax	vacation	

1. He waves a cape. Who is he?

He's a _____matador_____.

2. If you say "please," what do you have?

You have good _____manners_____.

3. If you sit and rest, what do you do?

You _____relax_____.

4. You won't see any hills here. Where are you?

You are on the _____plains_____.

5. You go on this for fun. What is it?

It's a _____vacation_____.

6. If you roped a cow, what did you do?

You _____captured_____ it.

7. What do you use to think about new things?

You use your _____imagination_____.

TRY THIS! On a separate sheet of paper, make up new riddles for two of the Vocabulary Words. Then give your riddles to a classmate to see if he or she can solve them.

© Harcourt

Practice Book
Banner Days

Name _____

Skill Reminder • A describing word tells about a
noun. Some describing words tell about color, size, or shape.

▶ Read the words under each line. Choose the describing
word. Write it on the line.

1. I am a _____ *tall* _____ cowboy.
   (take   tall   talk)

2. I have a _____ *big* _____ hat.
   (big   bark   bus)

3. I wear _____ *black* _____ boots.
   (by   black   blow)

4. I ride a _____ *brown* _____ horse.
   (bird   brown   build)

5. I have a _____ *long* _____ rope.
   (long   lunch   land)

6. I can make a _____ *round* _____ loop with my rope.
   (run   round   race)

7. Those _____ *white* _____ cows are mine.
   (when   white   went)

TRY THIS! Write three sentences about yourself. Use a describing
word in each sentence. Then draw a picture to go with your
sentences.

Name _____

How I Spent My
Summer Vacation

Vowel Diphthongs:
/oi/ oi, oy
TEST PREP

▶ **Find the word with the same sound as the underlined letters in the first word. Fill in the circle next to your choice.**

Example j<u>oi</u>n

    ⊙ toy

    ○ boat

    ○ top

1 c<u>oi</u>n

    ○ crown

    ○ room

    ⊙ boy

> 💡 **Tip**
> Say the word and listen to the sound that the underlined letters make.

2 enj<u>oy</u>

    ○ corner

    ○ book

    ⊙ point

> 💡 **Tip**
> Ignore any word choices that don't make sense.

3 b<u>oi</u>led

    ⊙ destroy

    ○ butter

    ○ bother

Practice Book
Banner Days

Name _____

▶ **Read the story. Then fill in the chart of causes and effects.** Possible responses given.

I had the day off from school. I was going to play soccer, but it rained. I stayed at home instead. I decided to give my dog a bath. We didn't have any dog shampoo, so I washed her with toothpaste. She seemed pretty clean, but her fur was kind of sticky. I had to give her another bath with human shampoo. Now her fur is shiny.

CAUSE	EFFECT
It rained.	The narrator stayed at home.
There was no dog shampoo.	The narrator washed the dog with toothpaste.
The dog's fur was sticky.	The narrator washed the dog with human shampoo.
The narrator washed the dog with human shampoo.	The dog's fur is shiny.

© Harcourt

SCHOOL-HOME CONNECTION Play a cause-and-effect game with your child. Ask your child what he or she would have done today if it had snowed, been sunny, or rained ice cream. Make up as many funny effects as you can.

Practice Book
Banner Days

Name _____

▶ **Write the words from the box that best complete the poem. Remember that the word you write should rhyme with the last word in the line before.**

| steer | reindeer | cheers | year | hear | beard |

I have a big sled over here.

It gets pulled along by eight _____reindeer_____.

Some people think it's really weird,

But I also have a big white _____beard_____.

Want a ride? Have no fear.

I know exactly how to _____steer_____.

I drive my sled both far and near,

But I only drive it once a _____year_____.

What's that noise, so loud and clear?

Those are reindeer hooves you _____hear_____.

If I can't drive, I shed tears,

But if I can, I yell out _____cheers_____.

SCHOOL-HOME CONNECTION With your child, choose three or four words from this exercise. Ask your child to see how many words he or she can think of that rhyme with them.

Practice Book
Banner Days

Name _____

▶ **Circle and write the word that completes each sentence.**

1. My favorite animal is a _____goose_____.
   green (goose) good

2. My favorite color is _____blue_____.
   balloon (blue) boys

3. You can see the _____moon_____ in the sky at night.
   (moon) main mop

4. His sister lost a baby _____tooth_____.
   tune tree (tooth)

5. A detective looked for a _____clue_____ to solve his case.
   (clue) cross crane

6. There is a bell on the _____roof_____ of the school.
   rope (roof) rake

7. The cowboy wore his red _____boots_____.
   (boots) branch bake

8. Mary used _____glue_____ to stick her cut outs to her paper.
   grade grass (glue)

18

Practice Book
Banner Days

© Harcourt

Name _____

▶ **Read the Spelling Words. Sort the words, and write them where they belong.**

Words with *oo*	Words with *ue*
1. _____ too	6. _____ blue
2. _____ zoo	7. _____ glue
3. _____ room	8. _____ clue
4. _____ rooftop	9. _____ due
5. _____ noontime	10. _____ true

Spelling Words

blue
too
glue
zoo
room
clue
due
rooftop
true
noontime
cowboys
voices
letter
sea
won't

▶ **Write the words that are left in alphabetical order.**

11. _____ cowboys	14. _____ voices
12. _____ letter	15. _____ won't
13. _____ sea	

© Harcourt

19

Name _____

▶ **Circle and write the word that completes each sentence.**

1. I mailed my letter at ____noon____.

    (noon)   note   noise

2. Are whales really ____blue____?

    (blue)   blow   blade

3. I want to know if that story is ____true____.

    tree   (true)   try

4. I will ask the man at the ____zoo____.

    zip   zero   (zoo)

5. I hope he sends me a ____clue____.

    coal   (clue)   coil

6. My library book about whales is ____due____.

    dry   drop   (due)

7. I need to hurry home to my ____room____.

    ramp   (room)   roam

8. I have to finish my book ____soon____.

    seen   shine   (soon)

9. I am so close to home that I can see the top of my ____roof____.

    ray   (roof)   raft

SCHOOL-HOME CONNECTION Have your child list the words from the lesson that have the o͞o sound spelled *oo* as in *moon*. Then ask your child to list the words that have the o͞o sound spelled *ue* as in *blue*.

20

Practice Book
Banner Days

© Harcourt

Name _____

▶ **Complete the labels for the pictures of Pam's vacation. On each line, write a word from the box.**

details	disappoint	forcibly
information	oceans	stroke

See the star I found? I didn't know stars

lived in **(1)** _____oceans_____ . I tried

to **(2)** _____stroke_____ its back.

I wanted to take my star home, but Mom

stopped me **(3)** _____forcibly_____ .

"I'm sorry to **(4)** _____disappoint_____ you,
but you have to stay here," I told the star.

"There are a lot of **(5)** _____details_____
about stars in my book, but there isn't any

(6) _____information_____ at all about stars
like you!"

 TRY THIS! There are many creatures that live in the ocean. Choose one and write three sentences about it, using as many Vocabulary Words as possible.

© Harcourt

21

Name _____

Skill Reminder • **Some describing words tell how something tastes, smells, sounds, or feels.**

▶ **Read the words under each line. Choose the describing word that tells how something tastes, smells, sounds, or feels. Write it on the line.**

1. Samantha likes ____sweet____ snacks.
   (saw   sweet   song)

2. Her cat likes ____salty____ snacks.
   (salty   say   seed)

3. Samantha eats ____crunchy____ crackers.
   (crunchy   cry   calm)

4. Her cat eats ____dry____ cat food.
   (door   dry   do)

5. Samantha likes to listen to her cat's ____loud____ purr.
   (loud   let's   lake)

6. She does not like her cat's ____sharp____ claws.
   (sick   sharp   sorry)

7. Most of all, she likes her cat's ____sweet____ smell.
   (sat   sweet   star)

8. Her cat likes to rub against the ____rough____ rug.
   (rough   read   roll)

© Harcourt

Practice Book
Banner Days

Name _____

Syllable Rule • Divide a compound word between
the two smaller words in it.
Examples: hot/dog   sail/boat

▶ Read the words in the box. Write each word in syllables.

heartache	backpack	sunshine	headband
floormat	blackboard	childcare	tonight
healthcare	highway	bookstore	football

Compound Words

1. _head/band_   5. _black/board_   9. _high/way_

2. _heart/ache_   6. _child/care_   10. _floor/mat_

3. _back/pack_   7. _health/care_   11. _to/night_

4. _book/store_   8. _foot/ball_   12. _sun/shine_

▶ Write a sentence for three of the words. Responses will vary.

13. _____

14. _____

15. _____

Name _____

▶ **Read the paragraph. Then choose the best answer to each question. Fill in the circle next to your choice.**

Leisha walked to the pond to look for her dog, Tricks. There were wet dog tracks leading from the pond to the grass. Leisha followed the tracks. Then she heard a bark. It was Tricks! He was soaking wet. She quickly pulled a towel out of her backpack.

1. Most likely, Tricks was wet because

- ○ he played in the sprinklers.
- ○ it rained.
- ○ he ran under a water hose.
- ◉ he swam in the pond.

> **💡 Tip**
> Reread the paragraph to make sure you have the important information.

2. Which part of the paragraph helped you with the first question?

- ○ Leisha walked to the pond.
- ◉ There were wet dog tracks leading from the pond.
- ○ Leisha followed the tracks.
- ○ She quickly pulled a towel out of her backpack.

> **💡 Tip**
> Reread the first question. Which sentence might tell how the dog got wet?

© Harcourt

SCHOOL-HOME CONNECTION Read a favorite story with your child. Help your child use story clues to make sentences about the characters and setting.   **24**

Practice Book
Banner Days

▶ **Read the story. On each line, write the missing letters *gn*, *kn*, or *wr* that will complete each word.**

I **(1)** _____ew this day would be special. Dad cut the cake

with a **(2)** _____ife. I **(3)** _____ote a special card for Grandma.

Mom said I am a good **(4)** _____iter. We all **(5)** si_____ed it.

My brother **(6)** _____ocked on Grandma's door. The surprise

was **(7)** un_____own to Grandma. She smiled when she saw the

kitten curled around my **(8)** _____ist.

SCHOOL-HOME CONNECTION Invite your child to write three original sentences using words from this lesson.

25

Practice Book
Banner Days

▶ **Complete the picture labels. Write a word from the box on each line.**

thief	wife	leaf	elf	shelf
thieves	wives	leaves	elves	shelves

1. Three _____wives_____ dance.

One _____wife_____ sings.

2. A _____leaf_____ falls.

Many _____leaves_____ stay on the tree.

3. An _____elf_____ wakes up.

Two _____elves_____ sleep.

4. Three _____shelves_____ are full.

One _____shelf_____ is empty.

5. A _____thief_____ runs away.

Two _____thieves_____ stay.

SCHOOL-HOME CONNECTION Have your child write the words from the lesson. Ask your child to use a blue crayon to circle the *f* in each singular word and the *v* in each plural word. Talk about how each word changed.

26

© Harcourt

Name _____

▶ **Read the Spelling Words. Sort the words and write them where they belong.**

Spelling Words

Ends with *f* or *fe*	Ends with *ves*
1. _____ elf _____	6. _____ elves _____
2. _____ leaf _____	7. _____ leaves _____
3. _____ life _____	8. _____ lives _____
4. _____ shelf _____	9. _____ shelves _____
5. _____ wife _____	10. _____ wives _____

wife
wives
leaf
leaves
elf
elves
shelf
shelves
life
lives
rooftop
true
bone
draw
whose

▶ **Write the words that are left in alphabetical order.**

11. _____ bone _____	14. _____ true _____
12. _____ draw _____	15. _____ whose _____
13. _____ rooftop _____	

© Harcourt

27

Name _____

► **Circle and write the word that best completes each sentence.**

1. I will bring a _____loaf_____ of bread to the picnic.

(loaf) loafs loaves

2. I think we need two _____loaves_____ of bread.

loafs (loaves) loaf

3. Anne's paints and crayons are on the two bottom

_____shelves_____ of the closet.

shelf (shelves) shelfs

4. Let's take the umbrella on the top _____shelf_____ in case it rains.

(shelf) shelfs shelves

5. Did you invite Anne's art teacher and his _____wife_____ to the picnic?

(wife) wifes wives

6. Yes, I asked all of Anne's teachers and their _____wives_____ and husbands to come.

wifes (wives) wive

7. Did you see the picture she drew of the two _____calves_____ in the barn?

calf calfs (calves)

SCHOOL-HOME CONNECTION Ask your child to draw a picture of a shelf with a loaf of bread on it. Then ask him or her to write a sentence about the picture. Ask your child to add shelves and loaves to the picture and then write another sentence.

28

© Harcourt

▶ **Complete the sentences. On each line, write a word from the paint jars.**

mimicked fussed pale admired notice haze

Jake liked the **(1)** _____ pale _____ colors in this painting.

"There's a blue **(2)** _____ haze _____ over the hills," he said.

In another painting, baby birds **(3)** _____ fussed _____ for food.

Jake **(4)** _____ mimicked _____ the mother bird. "Did you

(5) _____ notice _____ how real that apple looks?" Jake asked. Can

you guess which painting Jake **(6)** _____ admired _____ most of all?

TRY THIS! Write three sentences about a person you admire. Use as many Vocabulary Words as possible. Draw a picture to go with your sentences.

Skill Reminder • **Some describing words tell how many.**

▶ **In each sentence, circle the describing word that tells how many. Then think of another describing word that tells how many. Write your new sentence.** Exact wording may vary.

1. Three boys row on the lake.

Six boys row on the lake.

2. Two grown-ups help them.

Five grown-ups help them.

3. They have three fishing poles.

They have nine fishing poles.

4. They want to catch seven fish.

They want to catch twenty fish.

5. There are five other boats on the lake.

There are eight other boats on the lake.

6. Four girls swim in the lake.

Two girls swim in the lake.

7. Ten children fish from the shore.

Four children fish from the shore.

8. Seven ducks swim by.

Twelve ducks swim by.

© Harcourt

Practice Book
Banner Days

| Syllable Rule | • **Divide a compound word between the two smaller words in it.** |

Examples: hot/dog   sail/boat

▶ Read the words in the box. Write each word in syllables. Use slash marks to separate the syllables.

birthday	broadcast	catfish	sidewalk
daydream	cowboy	sunshine	horseshoe
rainbow	pinpoint	moonlight	bookstore

Compound Words

1. _____birth/day_____   5. _____day/dream_____   9. _____side/walk_____

2. _____cat/fish_____   6. _____broad/cast_____   10. _____sun/shine_____

3. _____horse/shoe_____   7. _____pin/point_____   11. _____rain/bow_____

4. _____cow/boy_____   8. _____book/store_____   12. _____moon/light_____

Name _____

▶ **Read the paragraph. Then choose the best answer to each question. Fill in the circle next to your choice.**

Judy liked to paint. She painted pictures of her family on paper. She painted a picture of a <u>happy</u> frog with a smile on his face. She painted a <u>light</u> blue star on a dark blue chair. Then she tried to paint a beard on her father. That's when her parents took her paints away. Now Judy uses crayons.

1. An antonym for *happy* is—

○ joyful

○ glad

◐ sad

○ merry

 Tip
Look for a word with the opposite meaning.

2. An antonym for *light* is—

◐ dark

○ clear

○ white

○ bright

Tip
Be sure to fill in the circle completely.

© Harcourt

🚒 **SCHOOL-HOME CONNECTION** With your child, make a list of a few words and their antonyms. Discuss the differences between the meanings.

Practice Book
Banner Days

Name _____

▶ **Read the story. On each line, write the abbreviation that stands for the underlined word.**

I have a very busy life. Every <u>Tuesday</u> I ride my bike to Pine <u>Street</u>. I meet <u>Missus</u> Walker for my piano lesson. I practice hard for my recital in <u>August</u>. On <u>Wednesday</u> I play soccer in the park. My coach is <u>Mister</u> Reed. In <u>December</u> and January I go skating at the rink. Sometimes I like <u>Sunday</u> best. That's when I sleep late.

1. _____ Tues.

2. _____ St.

3. _____ Mrs.

4. _____ Aug.

5. _____ Wed.

6. _____ Mr.

7. _____ Dec.

8. _____ Jan.

9. _____ Sun.

© Harcourt

SCHOOL-HOME CONNECTION Have your child go on an abbreviation search and list any abbreviations he or she finds. Guide your child to check places like calendars, phone books, and appointment cards.

33

▶ **Finish the story. On each line, write a word from the box.**

standing	freezing	doing	slowly
swimming	eating	taking	actually

A Very Cool Dream

Last night I dreamed I visited Antarctica.

My family and I were **(1)** _____actually_____

staying in a hotel made of ice! "What will we be

(2) _____doing_____ first," I asked my dad. He said,

"We'll be **(3)** _____eating_____ our breakfast soon." My sister

wanted to go **(4)** _____swimming_____ in the pool. Later, we were

(5) _____standing_____ in the **(6)** _____freezing_____ wind. My

mom was **(7)** _____taking_____ pictures of us. Then I

(8) _____slowly_____ began to wake up. I was so cold! My

blanket had fallen off the bed!

SCHOOL-HOME CONNECTION With your child, write a funny story about a vacation. Have your child use words with *-ing* and *-ly* endings.

34

Practice Book
Banner Days

© Harcourt

Name _____

▶ **Read the Spelling Words. Sort the words and write them where they belong.**

Words with *ing*	
1. _____ doing _____	6. _____ standing _____
2. _____ taking _____	7. _____ freezing _____
3. _____ swimming _____	**Words with *ly***
4. _____ eating _____	8. _____ completely _____
5. _____ starting _____	9. _____ actually _____
	10. _____ slowly _____

Spelling Words

completely
actually
doing
taking
swimming
eating
slowly
starting
standing
freezing
leaf
leaves
important
nothing
dinner

▶ **Sort the words that are left by the number of syllables.**

One-Syllable Words	Two-Syllable Word
11. _____ leaf _____	13. _____ nothing _____
12. _____ leaves _____	14. _____ dinner _____
	Three-Syllable Word
	15. _____ important _____

© Harcourt

35

Name _____

▶ **Circle and write the word that best completes each sentence.**

1. I am _starting_ _____ to deliver newspapers.

start   stop   (starting)

2. I fold each newspaper _carefully_ _____.

careful   (carefully)   care

3. I am _earning_ _____ money to buy a book.

(earning)   earned   earn

4. I like _riding_ _____ my bike.

ride   (riding)   rode

5. I ride _slowly_ _____ down the street.

slowing   (slowly)   slow

6. I am _doing_ _____ a good job.

do   (doing)   did

7. My bag is _completely_ _____ empty now.

(completely)   complete   completing

8. I like _reading_ _____ my book about penguins!

read   (reading)   reads

© Harcourt

Name _____

▶ **Solve the riddles. On each line, write a word from the box.**

flippers	hatch	horizon
miserable	slippery	waddled

1. You walk on a wet floor and fall. Why?

The floor is _____slippery_____.

2. You are at the beach. The sun is going down. What do you

see? The sun is setting over the _____horizon_____.

3. Penguins do not have wings. What do they have?

Penguins have _____flippers_____.

4. You have a cold and can't go ice-skating with your friends.

How do you feel? You feel _____miserable_____.

5. A mother duck just laid three eggs. What will happen?

The eggs will _____hatch_____.

6. The ducklings walked toward
their mother. How did they walk?

The ducklings _____waddled_____.

37

Skill Reminder • **A describing word that ends with *er* compares one thing with another thing. A describing word that ends with *est* compares one thing with two or more other things.**

▶ Add *er* or *est* to the describing word in ( ). Write the new word on the line.

1. The air is _____colder_____ than the water. **(cold)**

2. This is the _____coldest_____ place on Earth. **(cold)**

3. This wave is _____higher_____ than that wave. **(high)**

4. That is the _____biggest_____ bird I have ever seen. **(big)**

5. The water is _____deeper_____ over here than over there. **(deep)**

6. That bird's egg is _____smaller_____ than this bird's egg. **(small)**

7. Summer is the _____warmest_____ time of year. **(warm)**

8. We climbed the _____tallest_____ hill of all. **(tall)**

TRY THIS! Draw a picture of three short animals that are different heights. Write a sentence about each animal. Use the words *short*, *shorter*, and *shortest* in your sentences.

© Harcourt

Name _____

▶ **Choose the word in which *ing* or *ly* is added correctly. Fill in the circle next to your choice.**

Example: win

- ○ wining
- ◉ winning
- ○ wineing

1 extreme

- ○ extremly
- ○ extremmly
- ◉ extremely

Tip
Ignore the choice that is clearly wrong.

2 run

- ◉ running
- ○ runeing
- ○ runing

3 trace

- ◉ tracing
- ○ traceing
- ○ traccing

Tip
Think about the rules before you choose.

© Harcourt

▶ **Read the book titles and their descriptions. Then answer the questions. Write your answers on the lines.**

All About Eggs	Bird Watching	Bird Tales
by *Annie Dune*	*by* *Emma Gordon*	*by* *Jeff Greene*
This book describes the eggs of many different birds. Photos are included.	This book gives information about where to find different kinds of birds. It includes maps and diagrams.	This book tells of a talking penguin and his adventures on the Arctic ice.

💡 Tip
Nonfiction gives information.

1. Which books are nonfiction?

All About Eggs and *Bird Watching*

_____

💡 Tip
Fiction sometimes includes things that could not happen in real life.

2. Which book is fiction?

Bird Tales

_____

© Harcourt

▶ **Read the story. On each line, write the plural of the underlined word.**

Carla has many **(1)** hobby. She likes to garden. She calls the plants her **(2)** baby. In the park, she likes to look at the **(3)** poppy. She knows that gardeners have many **(4)** duty. It is not easy to grow **(5)** beauty like these. Carla also likes to learn about different **(6)** country. She goes to **(7)** library to get books about them. She collects coins and has the most **(8)** penny.

1. _hobbies_ _____

2. _babies_ _____

3. _poppies_ _____

4. _duties_ _____

5. _beauties_ _____

6. _countries_ _____

7. _libraries_ _____

8. _pennies_ _____

© Harcourt

SCHOOL-HOME CONNECTION Ask your child to write three sentences with plurals. Then ask him or her to tell you the singular for each plural word he or she used.

Practice Book
Banner Days

Name _____

▶ **Finish the story. On each line, write a word from the box.**

remove	return	recycle	replace
recall	preheat	preschool	preview

A Trip to the Library

Mona wanted to **(1)** _____return_____ her mystery book to the library. On the way, she dropped off newspapers

in the **(2)** _____recycle_____ bin. She waved to the

(3) _____preschool_____ children playing in the park. The

librarian asked Mona to **(4)** _____remove_____ her bookmark.

"I want to **(5)** _____replace_____ this mystery book with another one," Mona said. "Would you like a

(6) _____preview_____ of our new books?" the librarian asked.

Mona couldn't **(7)** _____recall_____ when she'd had such an enjoyable day! At home, she asked her mom to

(8) _____preheat_____ the oven. She wanted to bake a cake for the librarian!

© Harcourt

SCHOOL-HOME CONNECTION Ask your child to choose four words from the box. Have your child write the words and circle the prefixes *pre-* or *re-* in each word. Ask your child to tell you what the words mean.

42

Practice Book
Banner Days

Name _____

▶ **Read the Spelling Words. Sort the words
and write them where they belong.**

Words with *re*	Words with *pre*
1. recall	6. prefix
2. recycle	7. preheat
3. remove	8. prepay
4. replace	9. preschool
5. return	10. preview

**Spelling
Words**

remove
return
recycle
replace
recall
preheat
prepay
preschool
preview
prefix
swimming
doing
maybe
near
park

▶ **Sort the words that are left by the number
of syllables.**

One-Syllable Words	Two-Syllable Words
11. near	13. swimming
12. park	14. doing
	15. maybe

© Harcourt

43

▶ **Finish the sentences. Write a word from the box on each line.**

| reread | prefix | remove | refill | recycle | preschool |

1. Very young children go to this school.

It's a _____preschool_____.

2. You do this when you are finished with

newspapers and glass jars. You _____recycle_____.

3. This is a word part at the beginning of a word. It's a

_____prefix_____.

4. You do this to your muddy boots before you go inside.

You _____remove_____ them.

5. You do this when you like a book so much you want to read

it again.

You _____reread_____ it.

6. You do this to your glass when you want

more to drink. You _____refill_____ it.

© Harcourt

Practice Book
Banner Days

Name _____

▶ **Finish the story. On each line, write a word from the box.**

caused	clasp	confused	cornered
objects	removes	typical	

1. Annie almost never

_____ her watch.

One day she left the

_____ open. This

_____ her watch

to fall off.

2. Her cat, Sammy, always

spots _____ on

the floor. "This isn't just a

_____ cat toy,"

Sammy thought.

3. He picked up the watch.
Then it started to beep!
Sammy was

_____.

4. "Sammy!" Annie said. "You
have my watch

_____!"

© Harcourt

Practice Book
Banner Days

Name _____

The Pine Park
Mystery

Grammar:
Verbs That Tell
About Now

Skill Reminder • **An action verb tells what someone or something does. A verb can tell about an action that is happening now.**

▶ Read the sentences. Then read the words under each line. Choose the word that is a verb. Write it on the line.

1. I _____ sit _____ on the bench.
    (so sit stove)

2. You _____ walk _____ past the bench.
    (walk well way)

3. I _____ say _____ hello to you.
    (say she sea)

4. You _____ turn _____ around.
    (to turn tale)

5. We _____ talk _____ for a while.
    (talk two table)

6. Then we _____ go _____ to the swings.
    (good go green)

7. We _____ play _____ there.
    (pill play pond)

8. We _____ walk _____ home together.
    (walk white whale)

© Harcourt

Practice Book
Banner Days

Syllable Rule • Divide a word between the
prefix and the base word.
Examples: re/read   un/kind

▶ Add a prefix to the base word to create a new word that
makes sense in the sentence. Write the new word on the
line, dividing it into syllables.

1. We plan to _____pre/view_____ the new movie.

view

pre-   un-

2. I hope to _____re/visit_____ my old hometown.

visit

re-   un-

3. Ben was _____un/wise_____ to stay up so late.

wise

un-   pre-

4. She _____un/folds_____ her napkin to eat dinner.

fold

pre-   un-

5. We will _____re/turn_____ home after dark.

turn

un-   re-

© Harcourt

Name _____

▶ **Read the story. Then choose the best answer to each question. Fill in the circle next to your choice.**

The Mystery of the Missing Baseball Glove

John could not find his baseball glove. His game was in an hour. He ran all around the house looking for the glove. He looked under his bed. He looked under the table. Finally, he looked under his cat, Smoke. Smoke was sleeping on the glove!

1. What is the problem in this story's plot? ——
- ○ John likes to play baseball.
- ○ John has a cat named Smoke.
- ○ John has a baseball game.
- ◐ John lost his baseball glove.

> **Tip**
> Reread the story to help you find the answer.

2. How is the problem solved? ——
- ○ John finds the glove under his bed.
- ○ John finds the glove under the table.
- ◐ John finds the glove under the cat.
- ○ John finds the glove in his backpack.

> **Tip**
> Carefully read each answer choice.

© Harcourt

SCHOOL-HOME CONNECTION With your child, make up a story about someone who has lost something. Ask your child to tell you the story's main problem and how it is solved.

48

Practice Book
Banner Days

▶ **Write the word from the box that best completes each sentence in the story.**

| misplaced | underline | underdog | underfed |

A Doggy Tale

Nancy **(1)** _____misplaced_____ her favorite pen. She used the pen

to **(2)** _____underline_____ words she liked. Instead of finding her

pen, Nancy found a hungry, and **(3)** _____underfed_____ puppy.
Nancy took the puppy home and fed it. The dog got strong and
frisky. "You were unlucky, " Nancy said to her puppy. "Now you
have a family that loves you. You are an

(4) _____underdog_____ that won!"

SCHOOL-HOME CONNECTION With your child,
make a list of words that begin with *mis-* or *under-*.
Circle the base word in each word. Ask your child to
choose three words, and write two sentences for
each word, using the base word in one sentence and
the word with a prefix in the second sentence.

Practice Book
Banner Days

Name _____

▶ **Circle the best answer to each riddle.**

1. You have one above each eye.   bring (brow) bray

2. A circle is this shape.   (round) rained road

3. This is something you hear.   (sound) send sand

4. Rain falls from this.   could (cloud) called

5. People live in this.   hands horse (house)

6. This is used to make bread.   flare flyer (flour)

7. You use this to speak.   math (mouth) moth

8. This is a kind of bird.   oil (owl) only

9. This tells how something could sound.   land laid (loud)

10. It is a small animal.   (mouse) moist moose

SCHOOL-HOME CONNECTION With your child, make up a story about a mouse that lives in your house. Use as many words with the *ou* sound as you can.

Practice Book
Banner Days

© Harcourt

Name _____

▶ **Finish the story. On each line, write a word from the box.**

I'll	can't	don't	they'll
we'll	you'll	shouldn't	that's

Packing for Camp

"Tim, have you finished packing? **(1)** _____ They'll

be here soon," Dad said. "**(2)** _____ I'll be finished

in a minute," Tim answered. "I **(3)** _____ can't wait

to go. I just **(4)** _____ don't know if I should pack

my boots," he said. "Since **(5)** _____ you'll probably

ride horses there, you **(6)** _____ shouldn't forget your

boots," Mom said. "But I think you should wear them instead
of packing them." At last, Tim finished. "Well, I guess

(7) _____ that's it!"
he said. "And just in time, too!
The van is here!" Dad said.
"Have fun!" his parents called.

"**(8)** _____ We'll write you lots of letters!"

SCHOOL-HOME CONNECTION With your child,
discuss what you pack when you go on a trip. Ask
your child to use three contractions from the word
box in sentences that tell about packing.

51

Practice Book
Banner Days

© Harcourt

Name _____

▶ **Read the Spelling Words. Write the contractions in alphabetical order.**

Spelling Words

Contractions	
1. ____ can't ____	6. ____ shouldn't ____
2. ____ don't ____	7. ____ that's ____
3. ____ I'll ____	8. ____ they'll ____
4. ____ isn't ____	9. ____ we'll ____
5. ____ it's ____	10. ____ you'll ____

Spelling Words

we'll
I'll
you'll
they'll
don't
can't
isn't
it's
that's
shouldn't
preheat
recycle
shop
surprise
kittens

▶ **Write the words that are left in alphabetical order.**

11. ____ kittens ____	14. ____ shop ____
12. ____ preheat ____	15. ____ surprise ____
13. ____ recycle ____	

© Harcourt

Practice Book
Banner Days

Name _____

▶ **Circle and write the word that best completes each sentence.**

1. _____ give my teacher a party.

   Well   (**We'll**)   **We'will**

2. It _____ a good-bye party.

   (**isn't**)   **isnt**   **is'not**

3. _____ a "We Like You" party!

   It'is   **Its**   (**It's**)

4. _____ the best kind!

   (**That's**)   **That'is**   **Thats**

5. We _____ wait!

   cann't   **can'not**   (**can't**)

6. _____ get a cake.

   (**She'll**)   **She'will**   **Shell**

7. We _____ make noise.

   (**shouldn't**)   **shouldno't**   **should't**

8. _____ surprised!

   Shes   (**She's**)   **She'is**

© Harcourt

SCHOOL-HOME CONNECTION With your child, write the two words that make up each contraction above. Use the contractions in new sentences.

53

Practice Book
Banner Days

▶ **Complete the sentences. On each line, write a word from the box.**

addresses	clerk	grown	honor	pour	route

We Love You, Mrs. King!

We are having a party in _____honor_____ of Mrs. King.

She drives the bus on our _____route_____ .

My brother is _____grown_____ up now, but he used to ride Mrs. King's bus, too.

She must know the _____addresses_____ of hundreds of students!

I'll go to the store to ask the _____clerk_____ to order us a cake.

I'll _____pour_____ cold drinks for everybody.

 TRY THIS! Write sentences about a job you would like to have when you grow up. Use the Vocabulary Words in your sentences.

Name _____

Skill Reminder • **When the naming part of a sentence tells about one, add the letter _s_ to most verbs. Do not add an _s_ to the verb when the naming part tells about _I_, _you_, or more than one.**

▶ **Look at the verb in ( ). Decide if it needs an _s_ to finish the sentence correctly. Write the verb on the line.**

1. The mail carrier _____walks_____ down the street. **(walk)**

2. He _____brings_____ a package for two children. **(bring)**

3. Jan and Jesse _____want_____ to get the package. **(want)**

4. At last the package _____comes_____. **(come)**

5. The children _____open_____ the package. **(open)**

6. Jan _____gets_____ a box of cookies. **(get)**

7. Jesse and Jan _____like_____ all the presents. **(like)**

8. Jesse _____writes_____ a thank-you letter. **(write)**

 TRY THIS! Write a thank-you letter to someone who helps people. Tell that person why you like what he or she does.

Practice Book
Banner Days

▶ **Choose the word that is the correct contraction for the words. Fill in the circle next to your choice.**

Example **I am**

- ○ Iam
- ◉ I'm
- ○ Im

1 **he is**

- ○ hes
- ○ hee's
- ◉ he's

2 **let us**

- ○ lets
- ◉ let's
- ○ letts

> **Tip**
> Remember that you are taking out letters, not adding them.

3 **we will**

- ◉ we'll
- ○ wel'l
- ○ w'ell

> **Tip**
> Remember that the apostrophe (') is placed where a letter was taken out.

Name _____

▶ **Read the paragraph. Then answer the questions.** Possible responses are given.

Today there are two ways to write and send a letter. The old way is to write a letter on paper. The new way is to write e-mail on a computer. To send a paper letter, you put it in an envelope with an address and a stamp. The post office takes your letter to the address. To send e-mail, you press "send" and your e-mail goes to the other person's computer. For a paper letter, you have to buy a stamp. It does not cost anything to send e-mail. Both kinds of letters are ways to send a message to another person.

Name two ways e-mail and a letter written on paper are alike.

> 💡**Tip**
> Look for the word "both" in the paragraph.

1. _Both are ways to send a message to another person_

2. _Both are written messages_

> 💡**Tip**
> Reread the paragraph for details you may have missed.

3. Paper letters go through _____the post office_____, but

e-mail goes from your computer _____to another computer._____

4. You have to buy ___stamps___ to send ___paper letters___,

but e-mail is ___free___.

SCHOOL-HOME CONNECTION Gather some of your child's favorite toys. Ask your child to compare and contrast the toys.

57

Practice Book
Banner Days

© Harcourt

▶ **Read the story. On each line, write the form of the underlined word that makes the sentence correct.**

I have two **(1)** shelf on my wall filled with books. I like to read tales about the woods. Every fall I walk in the woods to find **(2)** leaf. I read about five **(3)** elf who live in the woods. One small **(4)** elves wore a **(5)** leaves for a hat. If I could find that hat, I would build a special **(6)** shelves for it! I would ask the elf what his **(7)** lives is like. Maybe he would tell me about the **(8)** life of all the elves!

1. _____ shelves _____

2. _____ leaves _____

3. _____ elves _____

4. _____ elf _____

5. _____ leaf _____

6. _____ shelf _____

7. _____ life _____

8. _____ lives _____

Practice Book
Banner Days

© Harcourt

Name _____

▶ **Complete the sentences. On each line, write a word with the same vowel sound as** *chew***.**

1. That shiny car must be _____new_____.
(seen   new   near)

2. We made a thick vegetable _____stew_____.
(sandwich   snack   stew)

3. Orange _____juice_____ is good for you.
(juice   candy   day)

4. The _____fruit_____ on the tree is ripe.
(fruit   leaves   light)

5. The pitcher _____threw_____ the ball fast.
(threw   ran   hit)

© Harcourt

SCHOOL-HOME CONNECTION Ask your child to draw and label pictures of a suit and a screw. Have your child underline the letters that make the vowel sound in each word.

Practice Book
Banner Days

Name _____

▶ **Read the Spelling Words. Sort the words
and write them where they belong.**

Words with *ew*	Words with *ui*
1. ___new___	6. ___bruise___
2. ___crew___	7. ___fruit___
3. ___stew___	8. ___pursuit___
4. ___grew___	9. ___juice___
5. ___threw___	10. ___recruit___

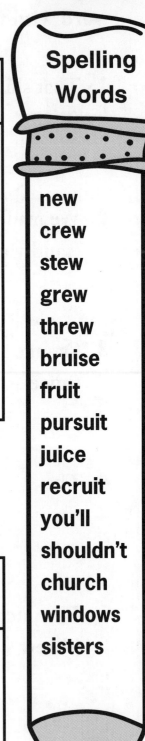

**Spelling
Words**

new
crew
stew
grew
threw
bruise
fruit
pursuit
juice
recruit
you'll
shouldn't
church
windows
sisters

▶ **Sort the words that are left by the number
of syllables.**

One-Syllable Words	Two-Syllable Words
11. ___you'll___	13. ___shouldn't___
12. ___church___	14. ___windows___
	15. ___sisters___

© Harcourt

60

Practice Book
Banner Days

Name _____

▶ **Solve the riddles. Write a word from the box on each line.**

new	juice	screw	grew	chew
crew	pursuit	threw	stew	flew

1. If a pitcher pitched a ball, he did

this. He ___threw___ it.

2. If a drum was just bought, it is this. It is ___new___.

3. When a plant got taller, it did this. It ___grew___.

4. This can be a drink made from fruit. It is ___juice___.

5. A thick soup is called this. It is ___stew___.

6. This means chasing someone. You are in ___pursuit___.

7. We do this when we eat. We ___chew___.

8. We use this to make a repair. It's a ___screw___.

9. These are the people who work on a boat.

They're a ___crew___.

10. When a bird went away, it did this. It ___flew___.

SCHOOL-HOME CONNECTION Ask your child to divide the words into two groups. Have your child list words spelled with *ew* in one group and words spelled with *ui* in the other group.

Practice Book
Banner Days

© Harcourt

Name _____

▶ **Finish the story. On each line, write a word from the drums.**

appeared

imitated

conductor

rhythm

created

startled

Jen asked Mr. Strong, the train **(1)** _____conductor_____, for

an old box. She **(2)** _____created_____ a drum by putting a lid on

the box. Slowly she began to beat out a **(3)** _____rhythm_____.

Boom boom–boom BOOM! The noise **(4)** _____startled_____ two
girls who were walking by. "I like that sound. Let's dance!" one of
them said.

Then a man and a woman **(5)** _____appeared_____. They

both **(6)** _____imitated_____ the steps the girls were doing. Soon all
the people on the street were tapping their feet!

 TRY THIS! Write a few sentences about the music you enjoy most. Use at least three Vocabulary Words.

© Harcourt

Name _____

Skill Reminder • **A verb can tell about action in the past. Add *ed* to most verbs to tell about the past.**

▶ **Look at the word in ( ). On the line, write the word to tell about the past.**

1. Yesterday Lee _____ walked _____ up to the door. **(walk)**

2. She _____ pushed _____ the doorbell. **(push)**

3. My big brother _____ opened _____ the door. **(open)**

4. Lee _____ asked _____ for me. **(ask)**

5. I _____ greeted _____ Lee with a big smile. **(greet)**

6. I _____ pointed _____ toward my room. **(point)**

7. Lee _____ rushed _____ by me to look. **(rush)**

8. She _____ wanted _____ to see my new drum set. **(want)**

TRY THIS! Write four sentences about something you did last week. In your sentences, use verbs that end with *ed*.

Practice Book
Banner Days

| Syllable Rule | In a word with the VC/V pattern, divide after the consonant when the first vowel is short. Example: lem/on |

▶ Read the words in the box. Then write each word, dividing it into syllables.

| civil | habit | model | shovel | study |

fin/ish

1. _____ civ / il

2. _____ hab / it

3. _____ mod / el

4. _____ shov / el

5. _____ stud / y

© Harcourt

Practice Book
Banner Days

Name _____

▶ **Choose the meaning the underlined word has in the sentence.**

1. The school band got to the park early.

   ○ to stop a car in a place

   ◉ an open place where people can play

   💡 **Tip**
   Notice that *park* can be an action word and a naming word. In which way is the word used in the sentence?

2. The air was <u>still</u> chilly.

   ○ quiet

   ◉ up to this time

   💡 **Tip**
   Which meaning makes more sense?

3. She drummed a fast <u>beat</u>.

   ◉ a regular rhythm

   ○ to win instead of someone else

   💡 **Tip**
   Think about what a drummer does when he or she is playing.

© Harcourt

SCHOOL-HOME CONNECTION With your child, make a list of words that have more than one meaning. Make up sentences with the different meanings.

Practice Book
Banner Days

Name _____

▶ **Write the words from the box that best complete the poem. Remember that the word you write should rhyme with the underlined word in the line above.**

voice	joy	toy	noise

Across the street there lived a ___boy___

Who played and played with just one ___toy___,

A tiny whale the boy called ___Roy___.

All day long Roy gave him ___joy___.

They'd run and jump with other ___boys___

And always make a lot of ___noise___.

Alone at night if the boy had a ___choice___

He would talk to his toy in a quiet ___voice___.

SCHOOL-HOME CONNECTION Discuss your
child's favorite toys and games. With your child, write
a short poem about a favorite toy. Remind your child
to use at least two words with the *oi* sound.

Practice Book
Banner Days

© Harcourt

Name _____

Anthony Reynoso:
Born to Rope

Consonant
Digraphs:
/f/, gh, ph

▶ **Finish the story. On each line, write a word from the box.**

petroglyphs	photo	telephone	paragraph
laugh	rough	cough	tough

Finding a Treasure

Alda climbed over the **(1)** _____ rocks.

It was **(2)** _____
getting up the mountain. Finally, she was
at the top. She was so happy she started to

(3) _____. At the top

she saw some rocks with **(4)** _____. Then

she took a **(5)** _____ of the carvings.
She ran down the mountain so fast that she started to

(6) _____. When she got home, she

called the book store on the **(7)** _____.
She bought a book on treasures. There was a

(8) _____ on petroglyphs and a picture
of the rock Alda had found.

SCHOOL-HOME CONNECTION With your child talk
about things that make him or her laugh. Encourage
your child to write sentences describing these things,
using as many *ph* or *gh* words as possible.

67

© Harcourt

▶ **Read the Spelling Words. Sort the words and write them where they belong.**

Words with *gh*	Words with *ph*
1. cough	6. graph
2. enough	7. paragraph
3. laugh	8. petroglyphs
4. rough	9. photo
5. tough	10. telephone

Spelling Words

paragraph
petroglyphs
photo
telephone
graph
laugh
cough
rough
enough
tough
pursuit
recruit
birthday
buy
dance

▶ **Sort the words that are left by the number of syllables.**

One-Syllable Words	Two-Syllable Words
11. buy	13. pursuit
12. dance	14. recruit
	15. birthday

© Harcourt

Name _____

▶ **Circle and write the word that best completes
the sentence.**

1. Roberto had a _____ cough _____ and stayed home.

   (**cough**) **camp** **corn**

2. He still had a _____ paragraph _____ to write for homework.

   (**paragraph**) **party** **petrograph**

3. He thought, "I have done _____ enough _____ for today."

   every (**enough**) **earning**

4. Roberto closed this book on _____ phonics _____.

   funny **phony** (**phonics**)

5. He did not finish his _____ graph _____ for math class.

   (**graph**) **great** **grass**

6. It was a _____ tough _____ choice to make.

   touch (**tough**) **teach**

7. He called his friend Pedro on the _____ telephone _____.

   telegraph **television** (**telephone**)

8. "May I borrow your book of funny _____ photographs _____?"
   Roberto asked.

   forever **phonetic** (**photographs**)

SCHOOL-HOME CONNECTION With your child make a list
of words that begin with the letters *ph*. Choose two words and
write a sentence for each word. Then have your
child draw a picture that tells about the sentence.

Practice Book
Banner Days

© Harcourt

Name _____

▶ **Finish the ad. On each line, write a word from the box.**

| dappled exhibition landscape business ranch thousands |

Come and stay for a week or two at Misty Meadow!

MISTY MEADOW

You will love your vacation at our

beautiful _____ranch_____. Ride a _____dappled_____ horse across the hills. Make a lasso and take part in a roping

_____exhibition_____. Walk in our new flower garden, cared for

by our own _____landscape business_____.

At Misty Meadow, you will feel you are _____thousands_____ of miles from the city!

© Harcourt

TRY THIS! Draw a picture of a place where you would like to go on vacation. Write two or three sentences about your picture. Use as many Vocabulary Words as you can.

Name _____

Skill Reminder • Some verbs tell what someone or something is like.

• *Am, is,* and *are* tell about now. *Was* and *were* tell about the past.

▶ These sentences tell about now. Write *am, is,* or *are* to complete each sentence.

1. This rope _____ is _____ big.

2. It _____ is _____ a gift for me.

3. I _____ am _____ very happy!

4. My horses _____ are _____ happy, too.

▶ These sentences tell about the past. Write *was* or *were* to complete each sentence.

5. Mr. Fox _____ was _____ my teacher.

6. Tasha and Sophie _____ were _____ in the class, too.

7. We _____ were _____ good riders.

8. I _____ was _____ the best!

 TRY THIS! Work with a partner. Take turns telling about yourselves. Use the verbs *am, is, are, was,* and *were.*

© Harcourt

Name _____

▶ **Choose the word that has the same sound as the underlined letters in the first word. Fill in the circle next to your choice.**

Example ne<u>ph</u>ew
- ○ niece
- ◉ five
- ○ review

1 lau<u>gh</u>
- ○ lazy
- ◉ phrase
- ○ gravy

2 tele<u>ph</u>one
- ○ television
- ○ bone
- ◉ enough

3 lau<u>gh</u>ing
- ◉ elephant
- ○ lacking
- ○ going

> **Tip**
> Be sure you know the sound the underlined letters make. If you are not sure about the sounds in one word, look down the page and find other words that you might know that have a **gh** or **ph**.

> **Tip**
> Say the first word aloud and listen to the sound the underlined letters make. Then read each answer choice and listen for the same sound.

© Harcourt

▶ **Read the story. Then answer the questions.**

Kit and Sunny

Kit had a horse named Sunny. Sunny was a beautiful black horse. It had a white star on its forehead. One day, Kit took Sunny out for a ride. When Kit rode past the town bank, she saw the robber, No Good Ned. Sunny and Kit chased the robber. He was running out with a sack of gold. Kit used her lasso to catch No Good Ned. Sunny and Kit saved the day!

1. Which sentence is important enough to put in a summary of this story?

Kit and Sunny caught a robber. *Or*

Kit's horse was black with a white star.

Kit and Sunny caught a

robber.

> **Tip**
> Remember that a summary tells what a story is mostly about.

2. Which sentence is **not** important enough to put in a summary of this story?

Kit used her lasso to catch the robber. *Or*

Sunny was a great horse.

Sunny was a great horse.

> **Tip**
> A summary tells only the most important events.

_____

© Harcourt

SCHOOL-HOME CONNECTION Read a short story or newspaper article to your child. Ask your child to summarize and retell the story.

Practice Book
Banner Days

▶ **Circle the best answer to each riddle.**

1. The sky is this color.   boil   blue   bell

2. This can stick things together.   goal   girl   glue

3. Twelve o'clock is this time.   nine   moon   noontime

4. You can visit animals there.   zoo   zip   zap

5. You use this to sweep.   broom   bring   broil

6. You use this to eat soup.   spoil   spoon   space

7. These men ride horses.   cook   cowboy   cool

8. If something is not false it is this.   true   tree   tray

9. A kitchen is one of these.   roof   room   roast

10. We use these to speak.   vases   voices   votes

SCHOOL-HOME CONNECTION Play *I Went to the Zoo* with your child. Start by saying, "I went to the zoo and I took my boot." Have your child repeat the sentence and add another word with the *oo* sound. Continue by taking turns naming appropriate items.

Practice Book
Banner Days

© Harcourt

▶ **Finish the story. On each line, write a word from the box.**

smarter	**tallest**	**smallest**	**fresher**
smartest	**taller**	**freshest**	

Grandma's building is **(1)** _____taller_____ than my house.

She lives in a city with some of the **(2)** _____tallest_____ buildings in the world. The food on our farm is

(3) _____fresher_____ than the food in the grocery store in the city. We grow our food in the garden. When my grandma visits

us, she says, "Han, you have the **(4)** _____freshest_____ food I

have ever eaten." Even though she has the **(5)** _____smallest_____ hands in our family, she can do almost anything. "You are the

(6) _____smartest_____ person I have ever met," I tell her. She gives me a hug and says, "When you grow up, you will be

(7) _____smarter_____ than I am."

SCHOOL-HOME CONNECTION Talk with your child about what life was like when you were in second grade. With your child, write sentences comparing how things were then with the way they are now. Encourage your child to use words with *–er* and *–est* endings.

75

Practice Book
Banner Days

▶ **Read the Spelling Words. Sort the words and write them where they belong.**

Spelling Words

Words with *er*	Words with *est*
1. _____taller_____	6. _____tallest_____
2. _____fresher_____	7. _____freshest_____
3. _____smaller_____	8. _____smallest_____
4. _____smarter_____	9. _____smartest_____
5. _____happier_____	10. _____happiest_____

taller
tallest
fresher
freshest
smaller
smallest
smarter
smartest
happier
happiest
paragraph
telephone
lion
oil
men

▶ **Sort the words that are left by the number of syllables.**

One-Syllable Words	Three-Syllable Words
11. _____oil_____	14. _____paragraph_____
12. _____men_____	15. _____telephone_____
Two-Syllable Words	
13. _____lion_____	

© Harcourt

Name _____

▶ **Circle and write the word that best completes the sentence.**

1. Chinese New Year is the _____happiest_____ day of the year for my family. **happy   happier   (happiest)**

2. On that day my grandmother looks _____happier_____ than anyone. **happy   (happier)   happiest**

3. We eat a _____bigger_____ lunch than we usually do. **big   (bigger)   biggest**

4. My grandmother cooks the _____freshest_____ crabs she can find. **fresh   fresher   (freshest)**

5. My brother, Wen, tells the _____funniest_____ stories he knows. **funny   funnier   (funniest)**

6. Then we make banners _____longer_____ than two yardsticks. **long   (longer)   longest**

7. At night we have the _____largest_____ parade I've ever seen. **large   larger   (largest)**

8. We dress up in the _____brightest_____ costumes. **bright   brighter   (brightest)**

9. My uncle wears a dragon mask with a _____wider_____ mouth than his own. **wide   (wider)   widest**

SCHOOL-HOME CONNECTION Talk about a custom or holiday that you and your child enjoy. Ask your child to write sentences describing what he or she likes. Have your child use comparing words that end in –er and –est.

77

Practice Book
Banner Days

© Harcourt

► **Complete the sentences. On each line, write a word from the box.**

celebrations	develop	furious
graceful	grocery store	students

1. Mom wanted me to get two cakes from the

_____grocery store_____ .

2. We were having parties for two

_____students_____ in my school.

3. I was _____furious_____

when one cake fell on my way home!

4. I had to get another cake so the

_____celebrations_____ could go on.

5. We worked hard to _____develop_____

a list of games we could play.

6. At the parties, some of us did

_____graceful_____ cartwheels.

 TRY THIS! Draw a picture of yourself with a friend at a birthday party. Write about your picture. Use as many Vocabulary Words from the box as you can.

Practice Book
Banner Days

Name _____

Skill Reminder • *Has* and *have* tell about now.
Had tells about the past.

▶ **Complete the sentences. Write** *has*, *have*, **or** *had*
on each line.

1. Tasha _____ had _____ a great class last week.

2. Today she _____ has _____ new things to learn.

3. Her brothers _____ have _____ classes now, too.

4. Last week, they _____ had _____ a long class.

5. Now they _____ have _____ a shorter class.

6. Today the teacher

_____ has _____ a show after class.

7. The students _____ have _____ fun
watching the show.

8. Tasha _____ has _____ even
more fun in class.

TRY THIS! Draw a picture of something that happened yesterday. Write
about the picture, using the verb *had*. Then write about the picture
as if it is happening now. Use the verbs that tell about now.

© Harcourt

79

Name _____

Syllable Rule   When a single consonant is
between two vowels, divide before the consonant.
Try the first syllable long. If the word makes sense, keep it!
Example: ti/ger   pa/per

▶ Circle the V/CV word that solves each riddle.

1. When you don't work, you are this.
   telegraph   sleeply   (lazy)   helpful

2. A small restaurant is called this.
   (diner)   café   store   more

3. You use a camera to take one.
   pots   floppy   (photo)   fitting

4. You use this to measure.
   yardstick   graph   (ruler)   grease

5. This is a type of bird.
   chicken   hawk   (raven)   robin

6. This is a day of the week.
   Sunday   Tuesday   (Friday)   Monday

7. You do this to a door.
   clog   (open)   close   keep

8. This is someone who rides.
   jockey   walker   (rider)   route

© Harcourt

Name _____

▶ **Read the paragraph and answer the questions.**

Chinese restaurants are popular all over the
United States. People like the many choices. You can get chicken,
beef, pork, or seafood mixed with all kinds of vegetables. You
can get vegetables and rice with no meat. You can get different
sauces. Another thing people like about Chinese restaurants is
the fast service. Most Chinese meals are cooked in a deep pan
with rounded sides. The pan, called a wok, cooks food quickly
and evenly.

1. Which sentence is an important
detail that supports the main
idea of the paragraph?

○ You can get a meal with
no meat at all.

○ You can get different sauces.

◉ People like the many choices.

💡 **Tip**

Find the main idea.
Then think about the
important details that
support the main idea.

2. Which sentence is an important
detail that supports the main
idea of the paragraph?

◉ Another thing people like
about Chinese restaurants
is the fast service.

○ Meals are cooked in a deep
pan with rounded sides.

○ The pan, called a wok, cooks food quickly and evenly.

💡 **Tip**

Look for the more
general statements.

SCHOOL-HOME CONNECTION With your child,
tell the story of an adventure you shared. Decide
which details support the main idea.

Practice Book
Banner Days

© Harcourt

▶ **Circle the best answer to each riddle.**

1. This means very pretty.
   (beautiful)   bike   became   bake

2. This means full of thanks.
   think   (thankful)   thing   thin

3. A person who does not do things
   with care is this.
   carry   (careless)   crack   course

4. This means not good for you.
   handle   hold   (harmful)   himself

5. A person who does kind things is this.
   thank   through   (thoughtful)   three

6. Something that is not dangerous is this.
   healthy   hearth   harm   (harmless)

7. A person who has no fear is this.
   frightened   frown   (fearless)   funny

8. A person who is happy is this.
   (cheerful)   charm   check   careful

SCHOOL-HOME CONNECTION Discuss the
meanings of these words with your child. Have your
child write five sentences using as many –ful and
–less words as possible.

Practice Book
Banner Days

Name _____

▶ **Write the words where they belong in the chart.**

airport	airplanes	chair	careful	dare	share
rare	scare	hair	pair	stairs	stare

air

mare

__airport__

__airplanes__

__chair__

__hair__

__pair__

__stairs__

__careful__

__dare__

__share__

__rare__

__scare__

__stare__

SCHOOL-HOME CONNECTION With your child
make a list of *air* and *are* words. Ask your child to
choose two words and write a sentence for each.
Then have your child draw a picture to illustrate
each sentence.

83

Name _____

▶ **Read the Spelling Words. Sort the words
and write them where they belong.**

**Spelling
Words**

Words with *air*	Words with *are*
1. _____airport_____	6. _____careful_____
2. _____airplanes_____	7. _____dare_____
3. _____chair_____	8. _____share_____
4. _____hair_____	9. _____rare_____
5. _____pair_____	10. _____scare_____

airport
airplanes
chair
careful
dare
share
rare
scare
hair
pair
tallest
happier
boat
city
morning

▶ **Write the words that are left in
alphabetical order.**

11. _____boat_____	14. _____morning_____
12. _____city_____	15. _____tallest_____
13. _____happier_____	

84

Name _____

▶ **Circle and write the word that completes each sentence.**

1. In the morning Claire brushes her _____hair_____.

   (hair)   half   harm

2. Today, her family is going on an _____airplane_____.

   (airplane)   armor   artist

3. They are going to the _____airport_____.

   action   (airport)   actor   _____

4. Claire _____shares_____ a sandwich with her brother.

   shark   shorts   (shares)

5. She sits down on a _____chair_____.

   choose   (chair)   chat

6. The plane will soar through the _____air_____.

   are   oar   (air)

7. She flaps her arms like a _____pair_____ of wings.

   part   port   (pair)

8. "It would not _____scare_____ me to fly over the clouds," she says.

   (scare)   scar   score

SCHOOL-HOME CONNECTION Ask your child what it would be like to fly through the air. Encourage your child to write a sentence about how it would feel and what he or she might see. Have your child use words with *are* and *air*.

85

Practice Book
Banner Days

© Harcourt

Name _____

▶ **Finish the ad. On each line, write a word from the box.**

| flock | glide | harbor | soared | swooping |

Take a ride in one of Red's Ready Planes!

Have you ever **(1)** _____soared_____ across the sky? Have you ever seen a

(2) _____flock_____ of birds flying and wished you could fly, too? You can do it in one of Red's Ready Planes! You will

(3) _____glide_____ over the city. You will sail above the boats in the

(4) _____harbor_____. Call Red today.

Soon you will be **(5)** _____swooping_____ through the sky!

TRY THIS! Imagine that you are a bird flying high in the sky. Write about what you see. Use as many Vocabulary Words as you can in your sentences.

> **Skill Reminder** • The verbs *see* and *give* tell about now. To tell what *he, she,* or *it* does, add *s*.
> • The verbs *saw* and *gave* tell about the past.

▶ **Read the words under each line. Write the correct form of the verb to finish the sentence.**

1. Years ago, Ms. Torres ___saw___ a bus that she liked. **(see saw)**

2. She ___gave___ a man money and bought it.
(gave gives)

3. Now she ___sees___ the bus every day.
(see sees)

4. Other people ___see___ the bus, too.
(see sees)

5. The people ___give___ Ms. Torres some money.
(gives give)

6. She ___gives___ them a ride on the bus.
(gives give)

7. Last week, the people on the bus ___saw___ a parade.
(sees saw)

8. The parade ___gave___ everyone a thrill.
(give gave)

Name _____

▶ **Choose the word that has the same sound as the underlined letters in the first word.**

Example: h<u>ai</u>r

     ○ heart

     ◉ dare

     ○ rear

1 c<u>a</u>re

     ○ car

     ○ ear

     ◉ stair

> 💡 **Tip**
> Say each choice aloud. Be sure each word makes sense when you say it.

2 <u>ai</u>rport

     ○ artist

     ○ part

     ◉ shared

> 💡 **Tip**
> Listen to the sound as you say each choice to yourself.

3 squ<u>are</u>

     ◉ fairground

     ○ school

     ○ quiet

> 💡 **Tip**
> Be sure to fill in the circle completely.

© Harcourt

Practice Book
Banner Days

Name _____

▶ **Read the paragraph and answer the questions.**

Possible responses are given.

    Two men talked loudly. One man pointed at his watch and then looked at the door. He shook his head. Just then a third man walked through the door. The two men stopped talking and walked over to him. They pointed at their watches.

1. What do you think the two men are talking about?

_____

They are talking about the third man.

2. How do you know this?

_____

They stop talking and walk over to the man.

3. Is the third man late or on time?

_____

late

4. How do you know this?

_____

The two men point to their watches.

© Harcourt

SCHOOL-HOME CONNECTION With your child, discuss common occurrences at home, such as making dinner and getting ready for school. Ask what signals help your child infer what is going on.

89

Practice Book
Banner Days

▶ **Read the story. Write each underlined word in the correct column on the chart.**

I am <u>going</u> to the park. There is a <u>swimming</u> pool in the park. It is <u>actually</u> a lot of fun. Sometimes, the water is <u>freezing</u>. Then I wade into the pool very <u>slowly</u>. <u>Lately</u>, it has been very hot during the day. So I jump right in off the <u>diving</u> board. I am <u>really</u> a very good swimmer.

-ing	-ly
1. _____ going _____	5. _____ actually _____
2. _____ swimming _____	6. _____ slowly _____
3. _____ freezing _____	7. _____ lately _____
4. _____ diving _____	8. _____ really _____

SCHOOL-HOME CONNECTION Discuss activities that you and your child like to do together. Have your child write sentences using words with the suffixes –ing or –ly to tell about these activities.

90

Practice Book
Banner Days

© Harcourt

► **Write the words from the box where they belong in the chart. The words with *oo* go under *book*. The words with *ou* go under *would*.**

| look | could | hook | cook | boyhood |
| foot | childhood | stood | should | brook |

Book	**Would**
look	could
hook	should
cook	
boyhood	
foot	
childhood	
stood	
brook	

SCHOOL-HOME CONNECTION Ask your child to think of three things he or she would like to do. Then have your child write sentences about them, using the word *would*.

91

Practice Book
Banner Days

▶ **Read the Spelling Words. Sort the words
and write them where they belong.**

**Spelling
Words**

Words with *oo*	
1. ___look___	6. ___boyhood___
2. ___cook___	7. ___childhood___
3. ___book___	**Words with *ou***
4. ___foot___	8. ___could___
5. ___stood___	9. ___would___
	10. ___should___

look
could
would
cook
book
boyhood
foot
childhood
stood
should
careful
chair
mountain
state
America

▶ **Sort the words that are left by the number
of syllables.**

One-Syllable Words	Two-Syllable Words
11. ___chair___	13. ___careful___
12. ___state___	14. ___mountain___
	Four-Syllable word
	15. ___America___

© Harcourt

Name _____

▶ **Circle the word that best completes each
sentence. Then write the word on the line.**

1. At camp we _____ over an open fire.
   cold   (cook)   cup

2. When we hike we travel on _____.
   (foot)   fold   full

3. You _____ wear strong
   boots when you go hiking.
   (should)   stood   shush

4. There are lots of trees in the _____.
   would   will   (woods)

5. A stream is also called a _____.
   buck   broke   (brook)

6. I _____ on the top of the
   mountain.   sound   (stood)   soon

7. _____ at the bird in the nest!
   loop   (look)   lose

8. There are many places we _____ like to visit.
   wood   work   (would)

9. I will write a _____ about our adventures.
   brook   brick   (book)

SCHOOL-HOME CONNECTION Help your child
write a list of words that rhyme with *look*.

93

Practice Book
Banner Days

© Harcourt

► **Complete the sentences. On each line, write a word from the box.**

connects	distance	features	mapmaker	peel

1. A map tells you the _____distance_____ between two places.

2. A _____mapmaker_____ is a person who makes maps.

3. To picture making a flat map of the round Earth,

_____peel_____ an orange. Then lay the skin flat.

4. Cities and rivers are _____features_____ that some maps show.

5. Sometimes a line _____connects_____ two cities on a map. The line tells how far one place is from the other.

 TRY THIS! Write three sentences about a place you have visited. Is it far away? Did you enjoy yourself? Use as many Vocabulary Words as possible.

Practice Book
Banner Days

Skill Reminder • **The verbs *come* and *run* tell about now. Add *s* to *come* and *run* to tell what *he*, *she*, or *it* does.**

• **The verbs *came* and *ran* tell about the past.**

▶ **Read the words under each line. Choose the correct verb to finish the sentence. Write it on the line.**

1. Most people _____come_____ by train.
　　　　　　(comes come)

2. It _____comes_____ into town at noon.
　　(comes come)

3. The trains _____run_____ on time.
　　　　　　(runs run)

4. That man _____came_____ on a bike.
　　　　(came come)

5. Some people _____come_____ by bus.
　　　　　　(comes come)

6. The bus _____runs_____ on time.
　　　　(runs run)

7. Long ago, the bus _____ran_____ late.
　　　　　　(ran runs)

8. Sometimes people _____run_____ for the train.
　　　　　　(runs run)

95

▶ **Read the words in the box. Put the words in the box under the correct column. Write the words in syllables.**

butcher	trumpet	sandwich	basket
squirrel	children	slipper	hundred
princess	chestnut	daughter	scribble

VCCCV Words

sand/wich
_____

but/cher
_____

chil/dren
_____

hun/dred
_____

chest/nut
_____

daugh/ter
_____

VCCV Words

bas/ket
_____

squir/rel
_____

trum/pet
_____

slip/per
_____

prin/cess
_____

scrib/ble
_____

© Harcourt

SCHOOL-HOME CONNECTION With your child, look through a dictionary for several words with the VCCCV or VCCV patterns. Point out the syllable marks in the dictionary.

96

Practice Book
Banner Days

Name _____

▶ **Read the Table of Contents. Then answer the questions.**

The Best Bug Book
Table of Contents

1. On which page would you begin to find information on feeding bugs?

 Tip
Use your finger to guide you as you read.

- ○ page 1
- ○ page 5
- ◉ page 10
- ○ page 15

2. Which chapter would tell you the most about big bugs?

 Tip
Read each chapter title again.

- ◉ Chapter 1
- ○ Chapter 2
- ○ Chapter 3
- ○ Chapter 4

© Harcourt

 SCHOOL-HOME CONNECTION With your child, look at a table of contents. Have your child try to figure out what kind of information might be in the various chapters.

Practice Book
Banner Days

Name _____

▶ **Circle the best answer to each riddle.**

1. This is a word part.   preview   (prefix)   prepare

2. When you tell a story
again, you do this.   review   resend   (retell)

3. Do this to your shoelace.   resend   (retie)   retire

4. You may do this
to your suitcase.   recheck   (repack)   reread

5. Do this with library books.   (return)   repay   rewrite

6. You do this when you pay ahead.   prefix   repay   (prepay)

7. If your glass is empty, you
may do this.   rejoin   refold   (refill)

8. If you just closed the door, you
may do this.   rework   (reopen)   reuse

SCHOOL-HOME CONNECTION Review words that
have the prefixes *re-* and *pre-*. See how many other
words with those prefixes you and your child can
name.

Practice Book
Banner Days

© Harcourt

▶ **Finish the story. On each line, write a word from the box.**

| you | wound | through | youth | soup | group | routine |

Grandma's House

Sometimes I go to my grandmother's house. Every day that

I am there I follow the same **(1)** _____routine_____.

A **(2)** _____group_____ of my relatives
comes over for lunch. Grandma makes a big

pot of **(3)** _____soup_____ for us
to eat. If I were to cut my finger while
slicing the vegetables, Grandma would put

a bandage on my **(4)** _____wound_____. After lunch, my

grandmother takes me to the **(5)** _____youth_____ center to

play games. We walk **(6)** _____through_____ the woods to get

there. Next time I go, **(7)** _____you_____ should come
with me.

SCHOOL-HOME CONNECTION Help your child
make up a recipe for a crazy soup. Write down the
name of the soup and the ingredients.

99

Practice Book
Banner Days

© Harcourt

▶ **Read the Spelling Words. Write the words where they belong.**

Words with *ou*	
1. coupon	6. throughout
2. group	7. throughway
3. routine	8. wound
4. soup	9. you
5. through	10. youth

Spelling Words

routine
through
you
soup
group
wound
coupon
youth
throughway
throughout
childhood
should
able
board
seat

▶ **Sort the words that are left by the number of syllables.**

One-Syllable Words	Two-Syllable Words
11. should	14. childhood
12. board	15. able
13. seat	

© Harcourt

Name _____

▶ **Solve each riddle. Write a word from the box on the line.**

group	throughway	routine
wound	youth	throughout	soup

1. This is a path or a road that goes through

   something. It's a _____throughway_____.

2. This is a hot liquid with vegetables or

   meat. It's _____soup_____.

3. If you are young, you are in this.

   It's your _____youth_____.

4. If you traveled all around the country, you did this.

   You traveled _____throughout_____ the United States.

5. A cut is one of these. It's a _____wound_____.

6. If you traveled with many people, you traveled in one of

   these. It's a _____group_____.

7. If you do the same things every day, you have

   one of these. It's your _____routine_____.

© Harcourt

SCHOOL-HOME CONNECTION Help your child
make up a story about a trip he or she would like to
take. Write a few sentences about the trip. Use at
least two *ou* words.

Practice Book
Banner Days

▶ **Complete the sentences. On each line, write a word from the suitcases.**

companions   sturdy   cassette   luggage   relatives

We will need to write to Grandma Duck and lots of other _____ relatives _____.

Let's pack our things in our _____ luggage _____.

Are these shoes _____ sturdy _____ enough for hiking?

It's going to be a long ride, son! You may want to take your _____ cassette _____ player.

I'm bringing plenty of _____ companions _____ to keep me company!

 TRY THIS! Write about getting ready for a trip. Use as many Vocabulary Words as you can.

Name _____

Skill Reminder • The verbs *go* and *do* tell about now. When the naming part of a sentence is *he, she, it,* or a noun that names one person or thing, add *es* to *go* and *do*.
• The verbs *went* and *did* tell about the past.

▶ **Complete the sentences. Write a word from the box on each line.**

go	goes	went	do	does	did

1. Subway trains _____go_____ much faster than a person can walk.

2. A subway train _____does_____ not have to wait in traffic.

3. Yesterday, we _____went_____ on a subway ride.

4. We thought the driver _____did_____ a good job.

5. You must see how fast a subway train _____goes_____.

6. What can you _____do_____ if you miss a train?

7. Don't worry. Soon after one train _____goes_____, another train comes.

8. I am glad we _____went_____ on a subway ride.

103

▶ **Choose the word that has the same sound as the underlined letters in the first word. Fill in the circle of the answer you choose.**

Example: y<u>ou</u>thful

- ○ train
- ○ crow
- ◉ through

1 y<u>ou</u>

- ○ brook
- ○ young
- ◉ soup

> 💡 **Tip**
> Say each choice aloud and listen for the same sound.

2 tr<u>ou</u>pe

- ◉ throughway
- ○ trust
- ○ throw

> 💡 **Tip**
> You can ignore the choices that don't make sense.

3 thr<u>ou</u>ghout

- ○ throwing
- ◉ regroup
- ○ outgrow

▶ **Read each paragraph. Then answer the questions.** Possible responses given.

Puerto Rico is the best place for your vacation. You will love the sunshine and our beautiful beaches. Great food and friendly people make your visit special. In the evenings, you will want to dance all night to the wonderful music in our clubs. Bring your children and have a vacation you will always remember.

1. What is the author's purpose— to entertain *or* to persuade?

_____to persuade_____

💡 **Tip**
Think about the words the author uses to describe Puerto Rico.

2. What does the author want you to do— come to Puerto Rico *or* take a cruise?

_____come to Puerto Rico_____

💡 **Tip**
Reread the paragraph to check your answer

© Harcourt

SCHOOL-HOME CONNECTION With your child, look at an advertisement or newspaper article. Discuss with your child the author's purpose for writing the item.

105

Practice Book
Banner Days

Name _____

▶ Add *mis–* or *under–* to the words in the box. Write each new word where it belongs on the chart. Make sure the words you write make sense.

lead	place	stand	print	go
water	understand	ground	wear	spell

mis		under	
1. _mislead_		6. _understand_	
2. _misplace_		7. _undergo_	
3. _misprint_		8. _underwater_	
4. _misunderstand_		9. _underground_	
5. _misspell_		10. _underwear_	

▶ Write the word from the chart that best completes each sentence.

11. I always _misplace_ my keys.

12. The subway runs _underground_.

SCHOOL-HOME CONNECTION Write *mis–* and *under–* on several strips of paper or on index cards. Then write the words *lead, place, print, understand, spell, stand, go, water, ground,* and *wear* on others. Ask your child to match the prefix cards with the word cards to form words from this exercise.

© Harcourt

Practice Book
Banner Days

Name _____

▶ **Write the words from the box in the column
where they belong. Read your lists to a partner.**

lawn	crawled	taught	naughty	yawn	saw
draw	seesaw	daughter		paw	law

cl<u>aw</u>

c<u>au</u>ght

lawn	taught
crawled	naughty
yawn	daughter
saw	
draw	
seesaw	
paw	
law	

SCHOOL-HOME CONNECTION With your child,
make up nonsense sentences using as many of the
augh and *aw* words as possible. For example: "The
naughty lawn crawled onto the seesaw." Encourage
your child to play with the words.

107

© Harcourt

Name _____

▶ **Read the Spelling Words. Sort the words and write them where they belong.**

Spelling Words

Words with *aw*	Words With *au*
1. crawled	7. caught
2. saw	8. naughty
3. seesaw	9. taught
4. draw	10. daughter
5. lawn	
6. yawn	

crawled
saw
caught
seesaw
draw
lawn
naughty
taught
daughter
yawn
throughout
coupon
hole
night
story

▶ **Sort the words that are left by the number of syllables.**

One-Syllable Words	Two-Syllable Words
11. hole	13. throughout
12. night	14. coupon
	15. story

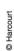
© Harcourt

Name _____

► **Write a word from the box to answer each riddle.**

lawn	crawled	taught	naughty
yawn	caught	saw	draw

1. You do this when you use a pencil to make a

picture. You _____ draw _____.

2. If you spotted an island, you did this.

You _____ saw _____ the island.

3. If your boat was stuck between two rocks, it was this.

Your boat was _____ caught _____.

4. Before you learned to walk, you probably

did this. You _____ crawled _____.

5. When you get tired, you do this.

You _____ yawn _____.

6. If you were bad, you were this. You were _____ naughty _____.

7. If you learned how to sail, someone did this. Someone

_____ taught _____ you.

8. This is the grassy place outside of a house. It's the

_____ lawn _____.

© Harcourt

SCHOOL-HOME CONNECTION Help your child make up a story about sailing. Use as many aw or augh words as you can.

Practice Book
Banner Days

▶ **Complete the sentences. On each line, write a word from the box.**

| cozy | drifted | fleet | launched | looming | realized |

1. On Saturday morning, Will ___launched___ his new boat.

2. "It's not part of a ___fleet___, but it will get there just fine on its own."

3. All day, Will's boat ___drifted___ slowly along.

4. Once he had to turn the boat almost sideways when he saw

a big rock ___looming___ in front of him.

5. By the middle of the afternoon, he ___realized___ that he must head for home.

6. "Boats are nice, but at night a ___cozy___ house is best," he said.

TRY THIS! Think about different ways to travel—boat, car, spaceship, skateboard. Use the Vocabulary Words to write sentences about your favorite way to travel.

Practice Book
Banner Days

Name _____

Skill Reminder • **A helping verb works with the main verb to tell about an action. *Has, have,* and *had* can be used as helping verbs.**

▶ **Complete the sentences. Write the helping verb *has, have,* or *had* on each line.** The helping verb *had* may be used in any sentence.

1. I _____have_____ not yet met the new captain.

2. The captain _____has_____ gone on many trips.

3. _____Have_____ you ever been on a boat?

4. Mr. Wicks _____has_____ never seen a whale.

5. He _____has_____ gone to sea many times.

6. I _____have_____ watched many boats sail on the water.

7. A big boat _____has_____ just now sailed near the shore.

8. I _____have_____ always liked sailboats the best.

TRY THIS! Write three sentences about an adventure you and your friends had in the past. Use a helping verb and a main verb in each sentence. Draw a picture to go with your sentences.

© Harcourt

Syllable Rule • **When two vowels come together in a word and have separate sounds, divide the word between the two vowels.**
Example: gi/ant

• **When a single consonant is between two vowels, divide before the consonant. Try the first syllable long. If the word makes sense, keep it!**
Example: ti/ger pa/per

• **If the word doesn't make sense, divide after the consonant and try it short.**
Example: drag/on vis/it

▶ Read the words in the box. Write each word where it belongs in the chart. Divide the words into syllables.

| silence | balance | writer | winter | madam | boa |
| neon | poet | melon | favor | shaken | trial |

ti/ger	gi/ant	vis/it
1. _si/lence_	5. _bo/a_	9. _bal/ance_
2. _wri/ter_	6. _ne/on_	10. _win/ter_
3. _fa/vor_	7. _po/et_	11. _mad/am_
4. _sha/ken_	8. _tri/al_	12. _mel/on_

© Harcourt

Practice Book
Banner Days

Name _____

▶ **Choose the correct word to complete each sentence.**

1. Please _____ me a letter when you take your boat trip.

○ right

◉ write

💡 **Tip**

Try to picture the correct answer in your mind.

2. The mouse's home was flooded by _____.

○ rein

◉ rain

💡 **Tip**

Think of the most common spelling of the word. Try that first.

3. Three mice and one mole made _____ small animals on the ship.

◉ four

○ for

💡 **Tip**

Think about the meaning of the word in the sentence. Then choose an answer.

SCHOOL-HOME CONNECTION With your child, make a list of a few homophones. Help your child draw a picture showing the various meanings of the words.

Practice Book
Banner Days

© Harcourt

Name _____

▶ **Read the story. On each line, write the two words that make up the underlined contraction.**

(1) <u>Isn't</u> it fun to learn something new? I **(2)** <u>don't</u> know how to play the piano yet, but **(3)** <u>I'll</u> soon learn. My teacher is good. **(4)** <u>She'll</u> help me learn to play. She says that you **(5)** <u>can't</u> practice too much. **(6)** <u>We'll</u> have a recital when I am ready. I **(7)** <u>shouldn't</u> complain about having to practice. **(8)** <u>It's</u> something that all musicians must do.

1. _____ is not

2. _____ do not

3. _____ I will

4. _____ she will

5. _____ can not

6. _____ we will

7. _____ should not

8. _____ it is

SCHOOL-HOME CONNECTION Ask your child to think of a musical instrument. Have your child choose three contractions from the story and use them in new sentences about learning to play that instrument.

Practice Book
Banner Days

© Harcourt

Name _____

▶ **Circle the answer to each riddle and write the word on the line.**

1. Something that is late is this.
override   **overweight**   (**overdue**)

_____overdue_____

2. Someone who frowns a lot might be this.
unimportant   (**unfriendly**)   **understanding**

_____unfriendly_____

3. A plane flies this way when you are below it.
overboard   (**overhead**)   **overdue**

_____overhead_____

4. You do this to a flag before you can raise it on the pole.
(**unfold**)   **unhappy**   **unheard**

_____unfold_____

5. When you pour too much water in a glass, it begins to do this.
overhead   **overnight**   (**overflow**)

_____overflow_____

SCHOOL-HOME CONNECTION Brainstorm words with *over-* and *un-* with your child. Then have your child guess the meanings of the words and write sentences for three of the words.

115

Practice Book
Banner Days

© Harcourt

▶ **Read the Spelling Words. Sort the words
and write them where they belong.**

**Spelling
Words**

Words with *over–*	Words with *un–*
1. overdue	6. unfriendly
2. overnight	7. unsure
3. overboard	8. uneven
4. overflow	9. unfair
5. overhead	10. unfold

overdue
overnight
overboard
overflow
overhead
unfriendly
unsure
uneven
unfair
unfold
daughter
yawn
hungry
group
above

▶ **Sort the words that are left by the number
of syllables.**

One-Syllable Words	Two-Syllable Words
11. yawn	13. daughter
12. group	14. hungry
	15. above

© Harcourt

Name _____

▶ **Finish the story. On each line, write the word from the box that completes the sentence.**

unsure	unfold	overnight	overdue	overhead

First Flight

"It's been months since I've had a chance to fly," said the

pilot. "My flight has been **(1)** _____overdue_____ for a long

time. "I have to make sure to bring my sleeping bag so I can

stay **(2)** _____overnight_____ when I land."

The pilot scratched his head. "My map is stuck together

and I'm **(3)** _____unsure_____ of where the airport is."

Just then an airplane flew above the pilot. "What's that

noise **(4)** _____overhead_____?" asked the pilot as he looked

up. "A plane!" he shouted. "Maybe that pilot can help me

(5) _____unfold_____ the map."

SCHOOL-HOME CONNECTION Together with your child, brainstorm a list of things that you can *unfold*.

117

© Harcourt

▶ **Finish the story. On each line, write a word
from the box.**

feat	heroine	hospitality
refused	spectators	stood

A noise startled Milly. Three young cats had fallen into the river

and were crying for help. Milly **(1)** ___refused___ to stand
by and watch. She jumped in and pulled them out. "Milly is a

(2) ___heroine___!" all the **(3)** ___spectators___ said.
"She saved Jack and his brothers!"

Jack told the crowd about Milly's **(4)** ___feat___.
"She saved three of us in one day. That tops a record that has

(5) ___stood___ for years," he said. Mrs. Cat gave a party

for Milly. Milly thanked Mrs. Cat for her **(6)** ___hospitality___.
"I was just helping my friends," she said.

TRY THIS! Draw a picture of someone doing a brave thing. Write four
sentences using Vocabulary Words that tell about your picture.

Name _____

Skill Reminder • A contraction is a short way to write two words. An apostrophe takes the place of the missing letter or letters.

▶ Read the sentences. On each line, write the two words that make up the underlined contraction.

1. <u>I'm</u> glad my dad likes model airplanes. _____I am_____

2. Every week <u>there's</u> a new model on the kitchen table. _____there is_____

3. When I get up in the morning, I <u>can't</u> wait to see whether Dad finished building another model airplane. _____can not_____

4. When <u>it's</u> raining, I can have fun indoors. _____it is_____

5. <u>That's</u> when Dad lets me help him. _____that is_____

6. I <u>don't</u> get bored at all. _____do not_____

7. Dad thinks <u>we're</u> a good team. _____we are_____

8. He says he <u>wouldn't</u> have as much fun by himself. _____would not_____

TRY THIS! Write three sentences about something you like to do after school. See how many contractions you can use.

Practice Book
Banner Days

© Harcourt

Syllable Rule • **Divide a compound word between the two words:** *shoe/lace.*

• **Divide between the base word and the prefix, the suffix, or ending:** *pre/view.*

• **Divide between two consonants that fall between two vowels:** *ham/mer.*

▶ Read the words. Write each word in syllables.

1. dollar _____ dol/lar _____

2. piglet _____ pig/let _____

3. problem _____ prob/lem _____

4. cowboy _____ cow/boy _____

5. fearful _____ fear/ful _____

6. preschool _____ pre/school _____

7. helpless _____ help/less _____

8. Sunday _____ Sun/day _____

9. unfold _____ un/fold _____

10. textbook _____ text/book _____

Name _____

▶ **Read the story. Then answer the questions.**

The weather was terrible. Heavy snow was falling in the city.
The ground was very icy. Linda, the pilot, looked at the dark sky.
This kind of weather could be very dangerous. The safety of the
passengers was most important. She knew what she had to do. She
could not fly the plane now.

1. Which sentence would go best
   at the end of the paragraph?

   ○ She must wait until the
      bad weather passed.

   ○ She must clean the
      airplane's cockpit.

   ○ She must fix the airplane's wings.

> 💡**Tip**
> Read the paragraph
> with each possible
> sentence at the end.

2. When the bad weather passes,
   the first thing Linda will
   probably do is

   ○ get on another airplane.

   ○ fly the plane.

   ○ park the airplane.

> 💡**Tip**
> Read all the choices.
> Choose the one that
> makes the most sense.

© Harcourt

SCHOOL-HOME CONNECTION Read a story to
your child that he or she has never heard. Have
your child guess the ending before you read it.

121

Practice Book
Banner Days

Name _____

▶ **Read the diary entry. On each line, write the underlined word in the correct column of the chart.**

Dear Diary:

I want to be a cowboy. I want to gallop along in <u>pursuit</u> of runaway horses. I even have a <u>new</u> saddle for my horse Star. I got Star when he was a pony. He <u>grew</u> up on our farm like me. Last summer I worked on a ranch. We worked hard. At night, we ate beef <u>stew</u> out on the range. We drank <u>fruit</u> punch. We called it <u>juice</u>. I want a <u>crew</u> of cowboys to <u>recruit</u> me today!

Your pal,

Luis

ew		**ui**	
1.	new	5.	pursuit
2.	grew	6.	fruit
3.	stew	7.	juice
4.	crew	8.	recruit

122

Practice Book
Banner Days

© Harcourt

Skills and Strategies Index

COMPREHENSION

Author's purpose 105

Cause and effect 7, 16

Compare and contrast 57

Details 81

Fact and fiction 40

Locate information 97

Make inferences 24, 89

Narrative elements 48

Predict outcomes 121

Summarize/restate information 73

PHONICS/DECODING

Consonant Digraphs
/f/ *gh, ph* 67, 69, 72
/n/*gn, kn* 25

Contractions *'ll, n't, 's* 51, 53, 56, 114

Nouns and verbs with and without
inflectional endings 6
-es (f to *v)* 26, 28, 31, 33, 58
-sies, -ies 41

Prefixes
mis-, under 49, 106
over-, un- 115, 117
re-, pre- 42, 44, 98

R-Controlled Vowels
/ar/ *air, are* 83, 85, 88
/ir/ *ear, eer* 17

Suffixes
-er, -est 75, 77
-ful, -less 8, 82

-ing, -ly 34, 36, 39, 90

Syllable Patterns
prefixes 47

VCCCV or VCCV 96

VCCV 120

VC/V 64

V/CV 80

VV, VCV 112

Vowel Digraphs
/oo/ *ew, ui* 59, 61, 122
/oo/ *oo, ue* 9, 18, 20, 23, 25, 74
/oo/ *ou, ou(gh)* 99, 101, 104

Vowel Diphthongs
/oi/ *oi, oy* 10, 12, 15, 66
/ou/ *ou, ow* 1, 3, 50

Vowel Variants
/ô/ *aw, au(gh)* 107, 109
/ŏŏ/ *oo, ou* 91, 93

Skills and Strategies Index

GRAMMAR

LITERARY RESPONSE AND ANALYSIS

SPELLING

VOCABULARY

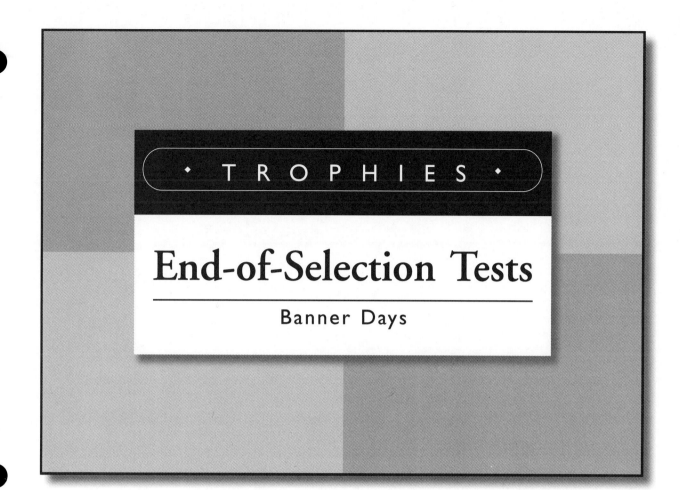

TROPHIES

End-of-Selection Tests

Banner Days

The Day Jimmy's Boa Ate the Wash

Directions: For items 1–18, fill in the circle in front of the correct answer. For items 19–20, write the answer.

Vocabulary

1. The egg did not hit Maria because she _____ .
Ⓐ sense   Ⓑ ducked
Ⓒ suppose   Ⓓ boring

2. Dad got a new _____ for our farm.
Ⓐ suppose   Ⓑ ducked
Ⓒ tractor   Ⓓ boring

3. That idea makes good _____ .
Ⓐ sense   Ⓑ boring
Ⓒ suppose   Ⓓ haze

4. Yes, I _____ you did your best.
Ⓐ ducked   Ⓑ suppose
Ⓒ tractor   Ⓓ numbers

5. Most stories are exciting, but that one is _____ .
Ⓐ ducked   Ⓑ suppose
Ⓒ tractor   Ⓓ boring

Comprehension

6. This book is most like a _____ .
Ⓐ poem   Ⓑ play
Ⓒ folktale   Ⓓ fantasy

Practice Book
Banner Days

Grade 2-2

7. What words does the girl use to tell her mother about the class trip?

Ⓐ exciting and fun   Ⓑ scary and dull

Ⓒ boring and dull   Ⓓ happy and fun

8. Why does the farmer crash his tractor into the haystack?

Ⓐ He isn't paying attention to where he is going.

Ⓑ He knocks it over so the class can play in it.

Ⓒ The cow is crying.

Ⓓ He wants to say hello to the class.

9. Why is the farmer yelling at the pigs?

Ⓐ The farmer wants them off the school bus.

Ⓑ The farmer wants to feed them lunch.

Ⓒ The cow is crying.

Ⓓ The farmer's wife is angry.

10. In this story, the pigs usually eat _____ .

Ⓐ hay   Ⓑ corn on the cob

Ⓒ eggs   Ⓓ whatever they can find

11. Why do the hens start flying around when they see the boa constrictor?

Ⓐ They are saying hello to the boa.

Ⓑ They are scared of the boa.

Ⓒ The boa tries to eat one of the eggs.

Ⓓ The boa hisses at them.

12. What does the girl tell about first in the story?

Ⓐ Jimmy drops his boa constrictor in the hen house.

Ⓑ A cow starts crying.

Ⓒ An egg breaks on Jenny's head.

Ⓓ Marianne throws an egg at Jenny.

13. What starts the odd happenings at the farm?

Ⓐ the farmer's wife screaming

Ⓑ Jimmy taking his boa into the hen house

Ⓒ students leaving their lunches on the bus

Ⓓ pigs getting on the school bus

14. Who is Mrs. Stanley?

Ⓐ the farmer's wife   Ⓑ the girl's mother

Ⓒ a parent of a student   Ⓓ the teacher

15. Why does the class leave the farm in a hurry?

Ⓐ Jimmy wants to leave his boa constrictor.

Ⓑ The bus driver says that they are late.

Ⓒ Their teacher is upset that the farmer's wife is screaming.

Ⓓ The farmer tells the class to leave right away.

16. Which word best tells what the class is like?

Ⓐ wild   Ⓑ shy

Ⓒ quiet   Ⓓ brave

17. Where does the girl's story take place?

    Ⓐ at the farm   Ⓑ on the school bus

    Ⓒ at the girl's house   Ⓓ at the girl's school

18. Why did the writer write this story?

    Ⓐ to give the reader something funny to read

    Ⓑ to tell what boa constrictors are like

    Ⓒ to talk about how to behave on a class trip

    Ⓓ to tell what farms are like

19. Think about the story's title. Tell why the farmer's wife is screaming.

_____

_____

_____

_____

_____

20. Is this story real or make-believe? Why?

_____

_____

_____

_____

How I Spent My Summer Vacation

Directions: For items 1–18, fill in the circle in front of the correct answer. For items 19–20, write the answer.

Vocabulary

1. If you _____, you will feel better.
Ⓐ relax   Ⓑ imagination
Ⓒ plains   Ⓓ captured

2. The cat _____ the mouse.
Ⓐ matador   Ⓑ captured
Ⓒ plains   Ⓓ vacation

3. My family went on a trip for our summer _____ .
Ⓐ imagination   Ⓑ manners
Ⓒ relax   Ⓓ vacation

4. Cowboys and cattle live on the _____ .
Ⓐ matador   Ⓑ captured
Ⓒ plains   Ⓓ manners

5. The author had a great _____ to write this story.
Ⓐ vacation   Ⓑ relax
Ⓒ captured   Ⓓ imagination

6. On the class trip, everyone showed good _____ .
Ⓐ matador   Ⓑ manners
Ⓒ plains   Ⓓ vacation

A5

7. The _____ waved a red flag at the bull.

Ⓐ captured   Ⓑ imagination

Ⓒ vacation   Ⓓ matador

Comprehension

8. Wallace went to his aunt's house aboard a _____ .

Ⓐ train   Ⓑ car

Ⓒ bus   Ⓓ wagon

9. Why do Wallace's parents send him out West?

Ⓐ They want some time alone.

Ⓑ They think that he will be bored at home.

Ⓒ They are worried that his imagination is getting too wild.

Ⓓ They want his aunt to teach him to read.

10. At first, Wallace thinks that the cowboys are _____ .

Ⓐ tough and noisy   Ⓑ mean and quiet

Ⓒ loud and mean   Ⓓ shy but friendly

11. Why do the cowboys capture Wallace?

Ⓐ They are angry at his aunt.

Ⓑ They are angry at his parents.

Ⓒ One of the cowboys is sick.

Ⓓ One of the cowboys has quit.

12. Think about Wallace's postcard to his aunt. How does Wallace feel about being carried off?

Ⓐ not afraid   Ⓑ homesick

Ⓒ mad   Ⓓ scared

13. Roping, riding, and making a fire with sticks are _____ .

Ⓐ ways to get to his aunt's house

Ⓑ things that cowboys do

Ⓒ things that cowboys wear

Ⓓ ways that his aunt tries to free him

14. When does Wallace get to see his aunt?

Ⓐ the day he arrives out West

Ⓑ the day he becomes a first-rate cowhand

Ⓒ the day he falls off his horse

Ⓓ the day the roundup is over

15. What terrible sight does Wallace see at his aunt's house?

Ⓐ Aunt Fern cooking a barbecue

Ⓑ a bull fight

Ⓒ cowhands dancing

Ⓓ cattle ready to stampede

16. The cattle charge at Wallace. In this story, <u>charge</u> means to _____ .

Ⓐ pay for later   Ⓑ rush toward

Ⓒ blame someone   Ⓓ ask the price

Grade 2-2

17. What does Wallace use for his "new kind of cowboying"?

   Ⓐ a tablecloth   Ⓑ fire

   Ⓒ a rope   Ⓓ his vest

18. When does Wallace write about his adventures in the West?

   Ⓐ in the summer   Ⓑ in the fall

   Ⓒ in the winter   Ⓓ in the spring

19. How does Wallace feel about the cowboys after he gets to know them?

_____

_____

_____

_____

_____

20. Is Wallace's story real or make-believe? Tell why.

_____

_____

_____

_____

_____

© Harcourt

Dear Mr. Blueberry

Directions: For items 1–18, fill in the circle in front of the correct answer. For items 19–20, write the answer.

Vocabulary

1. I hope I do not _____ you.
  Ⓐ disappoint   Ⓑ forcibly
  Ⓒ information   Ⓓ details

2. Many different fish live in the _____ .
  Ⓐ details   Ⓑ stroke
  Ⓒ meadows   Ⓓ oceans

3. I can find a lot of _____ about birds in this book.
  Ⓐ disappoint   Ⓑ oceans
  Ⓒ information   Ⓓ vacation

4. The author added many _____ to the story.
  Ⓐ details   Ⓑ disappoint
  Ⓒ information   Ⓓ stroke

5. My cat likes it when you _____ his back.
  Ⓐ stroke   Ⓑ details
  Ⓒ disappoint   Ⓓ forcibly

6. The farmer had to _____ put the pig in its pen.
  Ⓐ details   Ⓑ information
  Ⓒ disappoint   Ⓓ forcibly

Comprehension

7. "Dear Mr. Blueberry" has many _____ .

   Ⓐ letters   Ⓑ poems

   Ⓒ plays   Ⓓ jokes

8. You know Emily lives in Nantucket, Massachusetts because _____ .

   Ⓐ she tells Mr. Blueberry where she lives

   Ⓑ Mr. Blueberry likes Nantucket

   Ⓒ all whales live near Nantucket

   Ⓓ of the postmarks on her letters

9. Who is Mr. Blueberry?

   Ⓐ a friend   Ⓑ an uncle

   Ⓒ a neighbor   Ⓓ a teacher

10. What is the first thing that Emily does to help her whale?

   Ⓐ She feeds him breakfast.

   Ⓑ She puts salt in the pond.

   Ⓒ She strokes his head.

   Ⓓ She tries to make her pond bigger.

11. What is Mr. Blueberry's second reason Arthur cannot be a whale?

   Ⓐ Whales never get lost.

   Ⓑ Whales do not go near people.

   Ⓒ Whales are too big for ponds.

   Ⓓ Whales never leave oceans.

Grade 2-2

© Harcourt

Practice Book
Banner Days

12. How does Emily feel when Arthur jumps up and spurts water?

Ⓐ scared   Ⓑ happy

Ⓒ surprised   Ⓓ nervous

13. When does Arthur let Emily stroke his head?

Ⓐ when she takes him breakfast

Ⓑ after she names him Arthur

Ⓒ the day she puts salt in the pond

Ⓓ after she reads Mr. Blueberry's letter to him

14. When Mr. Blueberry writes that "whales are migratory," he means whales _____ .

Ⓐ stay in one place

Ⓑ cannot travel far

Ⓒ travel very far every day

Ⓓ travel every once in a while

15. Mr. Blueberry knows a lot about _____ .

Ⓐ whales   Ⓑ ponds

Ⓒ Emily's pond   Ⓓ Emily's parents

16. Emily thinks that Arthur left the pond because _____ .

Ⓐ the water was too hot

Ⓑ he was hungry

Ⓒ Mr. Blueberry took him away

Ⓓ Mr. Blueberry's letter made him migrate

17. How does Mr. Blueberry try to make Emily feel better after Arthur leaves?

(A) He says that she can help whales when she gets older.

(B) He tells her that Arthur isn't real anyway.

(C) He offers to help her find Arthur.

(D) He tells her that Arthur will probably come back.

18. Why is Emily sure that the whale at the beach is Arthur?

(A) He smiles at her. (B) He eats a sandwich.

(C) She strokes his head. (D) He waves good-bye.

19. Name two things that Emily feeds Arthur.

_____

_____

_____

_____

20. List two facts about blue whales that are in the story.

_____

_____

_____

_____

© Harcourt

Cool Ali

Grade 2-2

Directions: For items 1–18, fill in the circle in front of the correct answer. For items 19–20, write the answer.

Vocabulary

1. Jane _____ the pretty red bike.
Ⓐ mimicked   Ⓑ admired
Ⓒ fussed   Ⓓ played

2. We did not _____ that Tom had left the room.
Ⓐ pale   Ⓑ haze
Ⓒ notice   Ⓓ twitch

3. The baby _____ because he wanted to eat.
Ⓐ admired   Ⓑ mimicked
Ⓒ notice   Ⓓ fussed

4. Bob mixed white paint and red paint to make a _____ pink.
Ⓐ haze   Ⓑ notice
Ⓒ pale   Ⓓ mimicked

5. The children _____ the ducks when they said, "Quack, quack."
Ⓐ fussed   Ⓑ mimicked
Ⓒ haze   Ⓓ pale

6. We could not see the sun because of the _____ .
Ⓐ notice   Ⓑ pale
Ⓒ admired   Ⓓ haze

© Harcourt

Comprehension

7. "Cool Ali" is most like a _____ .

 Ⓐ nonfiction book   Ⓑ science book

 Ⓒ real story   Ⓓ folktale

8. What does Ali like to do?

 Ⓐ draw   Ⓑ sing

 Ⓒ dance   Ⓓ play

9. Why does Ali go outside?

 Ⓐ She wants to talk with Mrs. Frye.

 Ⓑ She needs to buy some sidewalk chalk.

 Ⓒ It is too hot to stay indoors.

 Ⓓ She wants to play with Ira.

10. When Ali goes outdoors, what is everyone thinking about?

 Ⓐ the heat   Ⓑ the coming storm

 Ⓒ the fussing babies   Ⓓ the cool breeze

11. How does Mrs. Frye show that she likes Ali's drawing?

 Ⓐ Mrs. Frye takes off her sandals and wiggles her toes in the pretend water.

 Ⓑ Mrs. Frye makes a newspaper fan for Ali.

 Ⓒ Mrs. Frye smiles and says thank you.

 Ⓓ Mrs. Frye splashes the pretend water on her face.

Grade 2-2

Practice Book
Banner Days

12. What does Ali draw to keep Ira cool?

Ⓐ the North Wind   Ⓑ a lake

Ⓒ a beach umbrella   Ⓓ a fan

13. Where does the story take place?

Ⓐ on a farm   Ⓑ in a city

Ⓒ at a beach   Ⓓ near the North Pole

14. What does Mr. Boyle do after Ali draws the North Wind?

Ⓐ complains there is too much wind

Ⓑ looks for the polar bear

Ⓒ puts his feet in Mrs. Frye's lake

Ⓓ pretends he is cold and makes his teeth chatter

15. Ali makes everyone feel cooler by drawing _____ .

Ⓐ a snowstorm   Ⓑ rain drops

Ⓒ polka dots   Ⓓ a polar bear

16. No one notices the rain because everyone _____ .

Ⓐ is too hot

Ⓑ is playing with the babies

Ⓒ is busy enjoying the snow

Ⓓ has gone inside the building

Grade 2-2

Practice Book
Banner Days

Grade 2-2

17. <u>Pinged</u>, <u>drummed</u>, and <u>hissed</u> are sounds that _____ .

Ⓐ a band makes   Ⓑ chalk makes
Ⓒ hot weather makes   Ⓓ rain makes

18. "Oh, no," Ali moaned. "Oh, no!" In this story, <u>moaned</u> means _____ .

Ⓐ washed away
Ⓑ made a low, sad sound
Ⓒ cheered loudly
Ⓓ said something over and over

19. What gives Ali the idea to draw a raging blizzard?

_____

_____

_____

_____

20. How does Ali feel about the rain? Why?

_____

_____

_____

_____

_____

The Emperor's Egg

Directions: For items 1–18, fill in the circle in front of the correct answer. For items 19–20, write the answer.

Vocabulary

1. The ducks _____ up to the children to get something to eat.
- Ⓐ hatch
- Ⓑ waddled
- Ⓒ miserable
- Ⓓ wanted

2. We are sad and _____ because our cat is lost.
- Ⓐ slippery
- Ⓑ hatch
- Ⓒ waddled
- Ⓓ miserable

3. A hen sits on her eggs until they _____ .
- Ⓐ hatch
- Ⓑ horizon
- Ⓒ miserable
- Ⓓ waddled

4. I saw the sun appear on the _____ .
- Ⓐ waddled
- Ⓑ slippery
- Ⓒ horizon
- Ⓓ miserable

5. The ice on the pond is cold and _____ .
- Ⓐ flippers
- Ⓑ slippery
- Ⓒ waddled
- Ⓓ horizon

6. A penguin does not have hands, but it has _____ .
- Ⓐ flippers
- Ⓑ slippery
- Ⓒ hatch
- Ⓓ horizon

Comprehension

7. In this book, Antarctica is called a big _____ .

Ⓐ meadow   Ⓑ lake

Ⓒ island   Ⓓ jungle

8. In this book, who lives on Antarctica?

Ⓐ many children   Ⓑ penguins

Ⓒ ducks   Ⓓ no one

9. In summer, the weather on Antarctica is _____ .

Ⓐ hot and sunny   Ⓑ cold and windy

Ⓒ rainy and hot   Ⓓ really nice

10. _____ penguin takes care of the Emperor penguin egg.

Ⓐ Granddaughter   Ⓑ Baby

Ⓒ Father   Ⓓ Mother

11. The female penguin is _____ than the male penguin.

Ⓐ smaller   Ⓑ sadder

Ⓒ bigger   Ⓓ tamer

12. The female penguin spends the winter _____ .

Ⓐ finding food for her baby

Ⓑ protecting her egg

Ⓒ swimming in the ocean

Ⓓ getting food for the male penguin

13. A father penguin keeps the egg warm by _____ .

Ⓐ sitting on it

Ⓑ putting the egg under its tummy

Ⓒ putting it on the snow and ice

Ⓓ putting it under the mother's tummy

14. How long does it take a penguin egg to hatch?

Ⓐ two days   Ⓑ two weeks

Ⓒ two months   Ⓓ two summers

15. Winter in Antarctica begins in _____ .

Ⓐ December   Ⓑ March

Ⓒ July   Ⓓ May

16. Penguins have _____ to help them keep warm.

Ⓐ no fat under their skin

Ⓑ feathers and fur

Ⓒ lots of fat under their skin

Ⓓ a big fur coat

17. A baby penguin is called a _____ .

Ⓐ hen   Ⓑ pup

Ⓒ child   Ⓓ chick

18. Every adult penguin has its own special _____ .

Ⓐ call   Ⓑ fingerprint

Ⓒ nose   Ⓓ whistle

19. Name two things a father penguin does to care for a baby penguin.

_____

_____

_____

_____

_____

_____

_____

20. How does a father penguin get food for his baby?

_____

_____

_____

_____

_____

_____

Grade 2-2

© Harcourt

Practice Book
Banner Days

The Pine Park Mystery

> Directions: For items 1–18, fill in the circle in front of the correct answer. For items 19–20, write the answer.

Vocabulary

1. Today is a _____ day because nothing special is going on.
Ⓐ caused   Ⓑ removes
Ⓒ typical   Ⓓ cornered

2. Close the _____ on your bracelet.
Ⓐ removes   Ⓑ typical
Ⓒ caused   Ⓓ clasp

3. The directions were so long we were _____ .
Ⓐ confused   Ⓑ objects
Ⓒ typical   Ⓓ caused

4. We have many _____ in the box.
Ⓐ removes   Ⓑ objects
Ⓒ typical   Ⓓ confused

5. Jill _____ her boots before she comes into the house.
Ⓐ objects   Ⓑ caused
Ⓒ removes   Ⓓ typical

6. The rain _____ the drawing to be washed away.
Ⓐ cornered   Ⓑ caused
Ⓒ confused   Ⓓ removes

Grade 2-2

7. It looked as if the cat _____ the mouse, but the mouse got away.

   Ⓐ cornered   Ⓑ typical

   Ⓒ objects   Ⓓ caused

Comprehension

8. When does this play take place?

   Ⓐ in the future   Ⓑ long ago

   Ⓒ in the present   Ⓓ in the winter

9. Where does this play take place?

   Ⓐ in front of a bookstore

   Ⓑ on a farm

   Ⓒ on a school playground

   Ⓓ in a town park

10. Who jogs in place?

   Ⓐ Mayor Pitt   Ⓑ Coach Lee

   Ⓒ Jeff   Ⓓ Chief Wilson

11. Why is Lan bored before she loses her bracelet?

   Ⓐ The weather is bad.

   Ⓑ She is not getting along with Jeff.

   Ⓒ There is nothing interesting to do.

   Ⓓ She doesn't feel well.

12. When does Chief Wilson realize his badge is missing?

Ⓐ after he wakes up from his nap

Ⓑ as he is talking to Miss Rosa

Ⓒ when he goes back to the police station

Ⓓ before he takes his nap

13. All the missing objects are listed on the sign except for the _____ .

Ⓐ charm bracelet   Ⓑ police badge

Ⓒ silver pin   Ⓓ whistle

14. Which is most important to Lan?

Ⓐ losing her bracelet

Ⓑ solving a mystery

Ⓒ finding a bicycle key

Ⓓ playing catch with Jeff

15. How are all the missing objects alike?

Ⓐ They are pieces of jewelry.

Ⓑ They are small and shiny.

Ⓒ Some are round and gold.

Ⓓ They are large and brown.

16. The runners crossing the stage obscured the key. In this play, <u>obscured</u> means _____ .

Ⓐ ran   Ⓑ found

Ⓒ hid   Ⓓ lost

Grade 2-2

Practice Book
Banner Days

17. When Chief Wilson says that the "thief isn't any*body*," he means that _____ .

Ⓐ the thief is not a person

Ⓑ the thief is more than one person

Ⓒ there is no thief

Ⓓ the thief is a famous person

18. The mynah bird has put all the stolen objects in _____ .

Ⓐ her cage   Ⓑ the bookstore

Ⓒ a pond   Ⓓ a tree

19. In Scene One, what is Miss Rosa looking for?

_____

_____

_____

_____

_____

20. Why does Lan want to go to the park again?

_____

_____

_____

_____

_____

_____

Practice Book
Banner Days

Good-bye, Curtis

Directions: For items 1–18, fill in the circle in front of the correct answer. For items 19–20, write the answer.

Vocabulary

1. Will you _____ the milk for me?
- Ⓐ grown
- Ⓑ honor
- Ⓒ pour
- Ⓓ route

2. Tell me the best _____ to the lake.
- Ⓐ route
- Ⓑ pour
- Ⓒ clerk
- Ⓓ grown

3. At the store, the _____ helped me find things.
- Ⓐ addresses
- Ⓑ clerk
- Ⓒ honor
- Ⓓ route

4. The little seeds have _____ into a big tree.
- Ⓐ grown
- Ⓑ addresses
- Ⓒ pour
- Ⓓ honor

5. Write the _____ of the club members in the book.
- Ⓐ honor
- Ⓑ route
- Ⓒ grown
- Ⓓ addresses

6. It is an _____ to meet the Mayor.
- Ⓐ addresses
- Ⓑ honor
- Ⓒ objects
- Ⓓ early

Practice Book
Banner Days

Comprehension

7. This book is most like a _____ .

Ⓐ poem Ⓑ play

Ⓒ science book Ⓓ story book

8. When does the story take place?

Ⓐ forty-two years ago

Ⓑ present day

Ⓒ last night

Ⓓ in the future

9. What is Curtis's job?

Ⓐ crossing guard Ⓑ mail carrier

Ⓒ mayor Ⓓ writer

10. People leave their gifts for Curtis _____ .

Ⓐ on their front steps

Ⓑ in his car

Ⓒ at his office

Ⓓ in their mailboxes

11. Max gives Curtis _____ .

Ⓐ a pencil sharpener

Ⓑ a small, fat book

Ⓒ candy

Ⓓ a bottle of aftershave

12. Curtis has been doing this job _____ .

   Ⓐ not very long

   Ⓑ for eight years

   Ⓒ for a long time

   Ⓓ for a year or two

13. People leave gifts for Curtis because _____ .

   Ⓐ it is his birthday

   Ⓑ he is retiring

   Ⓒ he is always on time

   Ⓓ he is going on a vacation

14. People throw a party for Curtis at _____ .

   Ⓐ his house

   Ⓑ the last house on his route

   Ⓒ his neighbor's house

   Ⓓ the first house on his route

15. People have a party for Curtis because _____ .

   Ⓐ they like him

   Ⓑ it is his birthday

   Ⓒ they want to dance and eat

   Ⓓ he just got a new job

16. After the party, Curtis dreams about _____ .

   Ⓐ his retirement   Ⓑ his vacation

   Ⓒ the party   Ⓓ people's addresses

17. Which word best tells what Curtis is like?

   Ⓐ lazy   Ⓑ jealous

   Ⓒ sad   Ⓓ friendly

18. Writing thank-you notes is _____ .

   Ⓐ thoughtful   Ⓑ brave

   Ⓒ selfish   Ⓓ silly

19. Why do people share "remembering" at the party?

_____

_____

_____

_____

_____

20. Why does Curtis know everyone's address by heart?

_____

_____

_____

_____

_____

© Harcourt

Max Found Two Sticks

Directions: For items 1–18, fill in the circle in front of the correct answer. For items 19–20, write the answer.

Vocabulary

1. The loud noise _____ the baby and made her cry.
- Ⓐ appeared
- Ⓑ startled
- Ⓒ imitated
- Ⓓ created

2. The moon _____ in the night sky.
- Ⓐ startled
- Ⓑ imitated
- Ⓒ created
- Ⓓ appeared

3. The _____ helped us find seats on the train.
- Ⓐ conductor
- Ⓑ appeared
- Ⓒ rhythm
- Ⓓ honor

4. We started to dance to the _____ of the music.
- Ⓐ created
- Ⓑ imitated
- Ⓒ appeared
- Ⓓ rhythm

5. We _____ a beautiful painting on the wall.
- Ⓐ created
- Ⓑ appeared
- Ⓒ startled
- Ⓓ conductor

6. The children _____ the cow and said, "Moo."
- Ⓐ created
- Ⓑ startled
- Ⓒ imitated
- Ⓓ appeared

© Harcourt

Grade 2-2

Comprehension

7. What is Max's grandpa doing?

Ⓐ listening to Max drum

Ⓑ washing the windows

Ⓒ sweeping the steps

Ⓓ raking leaves

8. Before Max starts drumming, he is _____ .

Ⓐ talking to his grandpa

Ⓑ helping his grandpa

Ⓒ sitting on the front steps

Ⓓ waiting for his mother

9. How does Max get the twigs he uses as drumsticks?

Ⓐ His grandpa gives them to him.

Ⓑ The wind knocks them down from a tree.

Ⓒ Max shakes a tree until they fall down.

Ⓓ Cindy, Shaun, and Jamal give the sticks to him.

10. Before Max drums on the cleaning bucket, he drums on _____ .

Ⓐ hat boxes   Ⓑ soda bottles

Ⓒ his thighs   Ⓓ the steps

11. When Max answers his grandpa with a "Pat . . . pat-tat. Putter-putter . . ." he is imitating the _____ .

    Ⓐ rhythm of the rain hitting a window

    Ⓑ sound of pigeons in flight

    Ⓒ beat of drums in a marching band

    Ⓓ church bells

12. What is Max's mom doing before she sees Max on the steps?

    Ⓐ shopping for food   Ⓑ cleaning windows

    Ⓒ working at home   Ⓓ shopping for hats

13. What does Max use from Cindy, Shaun, and Jamal for part of his drum set?

    Ⓐ garbage cans   Ⓑ soda bottles

    Ⓒ hat boxes   Ⓓ cleaning buckets

14. Which building is around the corner from Max's house?

    Ⓐ a school   Ⓑ a church

    Ⓒ a train station   Ⓓ a hat shop

15. What does Max's father do for a living?

    Ⓐ window washer   Ⓑ plays in a band

    Ⓒ train conductor   Ⓓ policeman

Grade 2-2

16. Max learns how to drum by _____ .

   Ⓐ listening to the world and copying its rhythms

   Ⓑ taking lessons from a drummer

   Ⓒ playing the rhythms that he makes up

   Ⓓ listening to drummers on the radio

17. This book is mostly like _____ .

   Ⓐ a folktale   Ⓑ a play

   Ⓒ a story book   Ⓓ nonfiction

18. Where does this story take place?

   Ⓐ in front of Max's house

   Ⓑ at the train station

   Ⓒ next to the church

   Ⓓ inside Max's home

19. How does Max answer everybody's questions?

_____

_____

_____

_____

20. What is the only word Max says in the story?

_____

_____

_____

_____

Anthony Reynoso: Born to Rope

Directions: For items 1–18, fill in the circle in front of the correct answer. For items 19–20, write the answer.

Vocabulary

1. We saw horses and cows at the _____ .
- Ⓐ landscape business
- Ⓑ thousands
- Ⓒ dappled
- Ⓓ ranch

2. We saw a black horse and a _____ one.
- Ⓐ dappled
- Ⓑ ranch
- Ⓒ thousands
- Ⓓ landscape business

3. The rocks have been there for _____ of years.
- Ⓐ exhibition
- Ⓑ thousands
- Ⓒ ranch
- Ⓓ appeared

4. Mr. Pat runs a _____ .
- Ⓐ dappled
- Ⓑ grown
- Ⓒ conductor
- Ⓓ landscape business

5. The children's paintings are on _____ in the school gym.
- Ⓐ thousands
- Ⓑ dappled
- Ⓒ exhibition
- Ⓓ appeared

Grade 2-2

Comprehension

6. This book mostly tells about _____ .

  Ⓐ getting a new baby in the family

  Ⓑ a Mexican rodeo

  Ⓒ working in a restaurant

  Ⓓ someone's life

7. Anthony is named after his _____ .

  Ⓐ cousin   Ⓑ mother

  Ⓒ father   Ⓓ uncle

8. Who is telling this story?

  Ⓐ Anthony's father   Ⓑ Anthony

  Ⓒ Anthony's mother   Ⓓ Anthony's grandfather

9. When does Anthony get his first rope?

  Ⓐ as soon as he can walk

  Ⓑ when he starts school

  Ⓒ as soon as he can stand

  Ⓓ when he turns three years old

10. The petroglyphs are carvings that _____ .

  Ⓐ are hundreds of years old

  Ⓑ are carved in the wall of a building

  Ⓒ are well known around the world

  Ⓓ tell a story Anthony understands

11. Guadalupe is always crowded at Easter because _____ .

Ⓐ artists come to paint the walls of buildings

Ⓑ a rodeo is held there

Ⓒ a Mission church holds a giant festival

Ⓓ the Yaqui Indians have ceremonies in town

12. What kind of food does Casa Reynoso serve?

Ⓐ Italian food   Ⓑ Yaqui Indian food

Ⓒ Mexican food   Ⓓ rodeo food

13. At his grandparents' ranch, Anthony does everything but _____ .

Ⓐ practice roping on horseback

Ⓑ celebrate his cousins' birthdays

Ⓒ play basketball

Ⓓ pose for family photos

14. What kind of student is Anthony?

Ⓐ He works hard at school.

Ⓑ He sometimes finishes his homework.

Ⓒ School is not important to him.

Ⓓ He likes only sports at school.

15. In Mexico, "the most famous charros are like sports stars here." Charros are _____ .

Ⓐ cowboys   Ⓑ basketball players

Ⓒ rodeos   Ⓓ teams of cowboys

Practice Book
Banner Days

16. How does Anthony feel about doing rope tricks?
  (A) It's too much work.
  (B) He's proud to work with his father.
  (C) He brags about it at school.
  (D) He'd rather play basketball.

17. At birthday parties, there is always a _____ .
  (A) clown   (B) rodeo
  (C) piñata   (D) charro

18. When does Anthony feel like a celebrity?
  (A) when he spins the rope with his teeth
  (B) when he performs in a show
  (C) when his mother watches him perform
  (D) when he poses for pictures with tourists

19. What does Anthony's father do on weekdays?

_____

_____

_____

20. How does Anthony feel about having a baby brother or sister?

_____

_____

_____

© Harcourt

Chinatown

Directions: For items 1–18, fill in the circle in front of the correct answer. For items 19–20, write the answer.

Vocabulary

1. We need to buy milk when we go to the _____ .
Ⓐ develop   Ⓑ furious
Ⓒ grocery store   Ⓓ graceful

2. We have many _____ during the year.
Ⓐ celebrations   Ⓑ furious
Ⓒ graceful   Ⓓ dappled

3. The man was _____ when the dog ate his lunch.
Ⓐ develop   Ⓑ furious
Ⓒ ranch   Ⓓ celebrations

4. The _____ have homework every night.
Ⓐ students   Ⓑ grocery store
Ⓒ develop   Ⓓ appeared

5. The dancers are _____ when they dance.
Ⓐ celebrations   Ⓑ develop
Ⓒ sideways   Ⓓ graceful

6. With practice you will _____ into a good ball player.
Ⓐ graceful   Ⓑ develop
Ⓒ furious   Ⓓ honor

© Harcourt

Practice Book
Banner Days

Grade 2-2

Comprehension

7. The child in the story lives with everyone **except** a

_____ .

Ⓐ mother   Ⓑ father

Ⓒ grandfather   Ⓓ grandmother

8. Who is telling this story?

Ⓐ Grandma   Ⓑ Mr. Wong

Ⓒ Mr. Chung   Ⓓ the child

9. How does the storyteller feel about his hometown?

Ⓐ furious   Ⓑ bored

Ⓒ proud   Ⓓ cornered

10. In this story a cobbler is the one who fixes _____ .

Ⓐ shoes   Ⓑ crabs

Ⓒ feet   Ⓓ handcarts

11. Who goes to the tai chi class?

Ⓐ graceful dancers

Ⓑ young and old students

Ⓒ children under 10

Ⓓ Grandma

12. Why does Grandma make medicinal soup?

Ⓐ Mother and Dad want some for lunch.

Ⓑ Grandma and the child are sick.

Ⓒ She thinks it will keep her strength up.

Ⓓ It is time to eat.

© Harcourt

13. At the outdoor market, the child can barely move because _____ .

   Ⓐ Grandma needs his help

   Ⓑ Grandma is ready to eat

   Ⓒ it is very crowded

   Ⓓ Grandma will eat all the crabs

14. The child takes kung fu lessons to _____ .

   Ⓐ play on Saturday

   Ⓑ learn a new dance

   Ⓒ develop body and mind

   Ⓓ learn how to cook

15. What does the child plan to do on New Year's Day next year?

   Ⓐ dance with the lion

   Ⓑ march with the older kids

   Ⓒ watch a tai chi exhibition

   Ⓓ beat the drums

16. A <u>wok</u> is _____ .

   Ⓐ hot, sizzling oil   Ⓑ a pan for cooking

   Ⓒ fresh seafood   Ⓓ a noisy restaurant

17. In this book, "Gung hay fat choy" means _____ .

   Ⓐ here comes the lion

   Ⓑ time for the celebration

   Ⓒ Happy New Year

   Ⓓ let's watch the lion dance

Grade 2-2

© Harcourt

Practice Book
Banner Days

18. This story takes place in _____ .

Ⓐ a restaurant

Ⓑ the park

Ⓒ a market

Ⓓ Chinatown

19. What does the child do to show he cares a lot for Grandma?

_____

_____

_____

_____

_____

_____

20. Name two places the child and Grandma pass on their morning walk.

_____

_____

_____

_____

_____

Abuela

Directions: For items 1–18, fill in the circle in front of the correct answer. For items 19–20, write the answer.

Vocabulary

1. A _____ of birds flew over the trees.
   - Ⓐ soared
   - Ⓑ flock
   - Ⓒ glide
   - Ⓓ harbor

2. Five big ships are in the _____ .
   - Ⓐ flock
   - Ⓑ glide
   - Ⓒ harbor
   - Ⓓ develop

3. The kite _____ over our heads like a bird.
   - Ⓐ soared
   - Ⓑ harbor
   - Ⓒ glide
   - Ⓓ furious

4. The pretty boats _____ across the water.
   - Ⓐ harbor
   - Ⓑ flock
   - Ⓒ glide
   - Ⓓ swooping

5. The bird came _____ down from its nest.
   - Ⓐ swooping
   - Ⓑ flock
   - Ⓒ soared
   - Ⓓ glide

Comprehension

6. "Abuela" is most like a _____ .
   - Ⓐ fantasy
   - Ⓑ nonfiction book
   - Ⓒ poem
   - Ⓓ play

Practice Book
Banner Days

7. Abuela is my mother's mother. She is my _____ .

   Ⓐ aunt   Ⓑ neighbor

   Ⓒ grandmother   Ⓓ friend

8. Who is telling this story?

   Ⓐ a bird   Ⓑ Abuela

   Ⓒ a young girl   Ⓓ Rosalba's father

9. When Abuela and Rosalba say <u>buenos días</u>, they are saying _____ .

   Ⓐ good morning

   Ⓑ I hear you

   Ⓒ it is hot

   Ⓓ goodnight

10. Abuela and Rosalba wave at people waiting for the bus. Then what do they do?

   Ⓐ circle around the Statue of Liberty

   Ⓑ race with sailboats

   Ⓒ take a short ride to the airport

   Ⓓ visit cousin Daniel

11. When Abuela and Rosalba "glide close to the sea," they are _____ .

   Ⓐ flying smoothly and easily

   Ⓑ flying slowly

   Ⓒ being blown by the wind

   Ⓓ riding in a plane

© Harcourt

12. What does Abuela's skirt become when she races the boats?

    Ⓐ a motor   Ⓑ the wind

    Ⓒ a sail   Ⓓ wings

13. Which fruits have Spanish names?

    Ⓐ papaya, banana, apple

    Ⓑ banana, plum, mango

    Ⓒ strawberry, grape, papaya

    Ⓓ papaya, banana, mango

14. Abuela first came to America by _____ .

    Ⓐ ship   Ⓑ plane

    Ⓒ train   Ⓓ bus

15. Why does Rosalba think her uncle and aunt will give them lemonade?

    Ⓐ Her uncle and aunt will be glad to see Rosalba and Abuela.

    Ⓑ Her uncle and aunt have a store.

    Ⓒ Her uncle and aunt own a lemon tree.

    Ⓓ Abuela likes cool lemonade.

16. What do the clouds look like to Rosalba?

    Ⓐ an airplane, a balloon, and a tree

    Ⓑ a cat, a bear, and a chair

    Ⓒ snow, a bear, and a bed

    Ⓓ an airplane, a balloon, and a bird

Grade 2-2

Practice Book
Banner Days

17. Rosalba's father works _____ .
- Ⓐ in a park
- Ⓑ on the docks
- Ⓒ in a tall building
- Ⓓ at the airport

18. Which sentence is true about Abuela?
- Ⓐ Abuela is afraid of flying.
- Ⓑ Abuela loves fun and adventure.
- Ⓒ Abuela has lived in America all her life.
- Ⓓ Abuela only speaks English to Rosalba.

19. Why is the Statue of Liberty important to Abuela?

_____

_____

_____

_____

_____

20. Do Abuela and Rosalba really fly or does Rosalba imagine it?

_____

_____

_____

_____

_____

Practice Book
Banner Days

Grade 2-2

Beginner's World Atlas

Directions: For items 1–18, fill in the circle in front of the correct answer. For items 19–20, write the answer.

Vocabulary

1. I will _____ the orange for you.
  Ⓐ distance   Ⓑ connects
  Ⓒ peel   Ⓓ features

2. The _____ draws symbols on the maps.
  Ⓐ features   Ⓑ distance
  Ⓒ connects   Ⓓ mapmaker

3. Grandma's house is a long _____ away.
  Ⓐ distance   Ⓑ connects
  Ⓒ mapmaker   Ⓓ peel

4. The branch _____ the trunk to the leaves of the tree.
  Ⓐ peel   Ⓑ features
  Ⓒ connects   Ⓓ distance

5. A physical map key shows the _____ on the map.
  Ⓐ mapmaker   Ⓑ distance
  Ⓒ connects   Ⓓ features

Grade 2-2

Comprehension

6. A _____ tells where north is on a map.

Ⓐ map key   Ⓑ scale

Ⓒ globe   Ⓓ compass

7. A map shows _____ .

Ⓐ how to get somewhere

Ⓑ why the world is flat

Ⓒ a bird flying

Ⓓ how to name an ocean

8. From space, you can see _____ .

Ⓐ that the Earth is flat

Ⓑ all the planets at one time

Ⓒ all the Earth at one time

Ⓓ half the Earth at one time

9. Mapmakers draw the Equator on a map to _____ .

Ⓐ add more lines for the globe

Ⓑ divide the Earth into North and South

Ⓒ divide the Earth into East and West

Ⓓ show the land and the seas

10. To understand the features on a map, use the _____ .

Ⓐ Equator   Ⓑ map key

Ⓒ globe   Ⓓ map scale

Practice Book
Banner Days

11. How are an ocean and a lake different?

Ⓐ A lake is smaller than an ocean.

Ⓑ One is water, and one is land.

Ⓒ An ocean is surrounded by land.

Ⓓ A lake is bigger than an ocean.

12. The largest island in the world is _____ .

Ⓐ Greenland   Ⓑ a peninsula

Ⓒ Europe   Ⓓ a forest

13. A large stream of water is a _____ .

Ⓐ desert   Ⓑ forest

Ⓒ river   Ⓓ pond

14. The author says the shape of North America is _____ .

Ⓐ like a triangle   Ⓑ like a square

Ⓒ like a circle   Ⓓ an ice cap

15. Central America _____ .

Ⓐ is in the Sierra Nevada Mountains

Ⓑ connects North America and South America

Ⓒ crosses the Rocky Mountains

Ⓓ is on the Equator

16. The largest city in North America is _____ .

Ⓐ New York City   Ⓑ Canada

Ⓒ Mexico City   Ⓓ Los Angeles

Grade 2-2

© Harcourt

Practice Book
Banner Days

17. A shortcut between the Atlantic and Pacific Oceans
is _____ .

    Ⓐ down the Nile river   Ⓑ up the Mississippi

    Ⓒ the Panama Canal   Ⓓ across Mexico

18. Ice caps can be found in _____ .

    Ⓐ South America   Ⓑ the Pacific Ocean

    Ⓒ the Caribbean Sea   Ⓓ Antarctica

19. On which continent do you live?

_____

_____

_____

_____

_____

_____

20. Is this book fiction or nonfiction? Tell why.

_____

_____

_____

_____

_____

© Harcourt

Dinosaurs Travel

Directions: For items 1–18, fill in the circle in front of the correct answer. For items 19–20, write the answer.

Vocabulary

1. We need a strong, _____ table to work on.
  Ⓐ relatives   Ⓑ companions
  Ⓒ sturdy   Ⓓ celebrations

2. A trip is more fun when you have _____ with you.
  Ⓐ companions   Ⓑ cassette
  Ⓒ sturdy   Ⓓ features

3. We can play tapes on the _____ player.
  Ⓐ cassette   Ⓑ sturdy
  Ⓒ companions   Ⓓ luggage

4. We saw many _____ at the party.
  Ⓐ luggage   Ⓑ relatives
  Ⓒ sturdy   Ⓓ protects

5. Dad put the _____ on top of the van.
  Ⓐ relatives   Ⓑ companions
  Ⓒ luggage   Ⓓ sturdy

Comprehension

6. What is not in the story as a way to travel?
  Ⓐ helicopter   Ⓑ boat
  Ⓒ plane   Ⓓ limousine

Grade 2-2

7. Books and maps can help you _____ .
- Ⓐ pack luggage
- Ⓑ buy a cassette
- Ⓒ learn about places
- Ⓓ visit relatives

8. Which item should you leave at home when you travel?
- Ⓐ your toothbrush
- Ⓑ shampoo
- Ⓒ a map of your route
- Ⓓ your pet snake

9. What is one good thing about traveling on foot?
- Ⓐ You may get blisters on your feet.
- Ⓑ You can see more sights.
- Ⓒ You can get to places very quickly.
- Ⓓ You need lots of things to help you do it.

10. If you travel by bicycle or skateboard, you _____ .
- Ⓐ don't need them in good working order
- Ⓑ should follow the rules of the road
- Ⓒ always need to go as fast as possible
- Ⓓ can make up your own rules

11. A good car game is _____ .
- Ⓐ looking at different license plates
- Ⓑ singing loudly
- Ⓒ playing catch
- Ⓓ collecting souvenirs

© Harcourt

12. How is traveling on buses and subways alike?

   Ⓐ They make a lot of stops.

   Ⓑ They mostly travel underground.

   Ⓒ They are always free.

   Ⓓ They have tour guides on them.

13. After you hear the words *All aboard,* the _____ .

   Ⓐ driver stops   Ⓑ train leaves

   Ⓒ plane lands   Ⓓ train stops

14. What does a conductor do on a train?

   Ⓐ drives the train

   Ⓑ decides where a train will stop

   Ⓒ serves food to people

   Ⓓ names each stop as the train gets close to it

15. One job the ticket agent for an airline does is to _____ .

   Ⓐ pick up trays after people eat

   Ⓑ carry people's bags

   Ⓒ sell train tickets

   Ⓓ look at people's tickets

16. In this book why is security important at an airport?

   Ⓐ to be sure no one brings dangerous things on the plane

   Ⓑ to check that everyone has a ticket

   Ⓒ to serve snacks and drinks

   Ⓓ to help fly the plane

© Harcourt

Grade 2-2

Practice Book
Banner Days

17. To help you remember your trip, you
should _____ .

   Ⓐ bring a bag   Ⓑ take pictures

   Ⓒ move your feet   Ⓓ stretch your legs

18. Which kind of travel do the words <u>take</u> <u>off</u>, <u>fasten</u>
<u>seat</u> <u>belt</u>, and <u>land</u> tell about?

   Ⓐ boat   Ⓑ train

   Ⓒ plane   Ⓓ subway

19. What does the author say may happen when you
leave your home?

_____

_____

_____

_____

_____

20. List two things that are good about getting home
from a trip.

_____

_____

_____

_____

Grade 2-2

Montigue on the High Seas

Directions: For items 1–18, fill in the circle in front of the correct answer. For items 19–20, write the answer.

Vocabulary

1. The little boat _____ on the water.
  Ⓐ fleet   Ⓑ cozy
  Ⓒ drifted   Ⓓ realized

2. Our home is warm and _____ .
  Ⓐ cozy   Ⓑ drifted
  Ⓒ looming   Ⓓ fleet

3. The _____ of ships sailed into the harbor.
  Ⓐ launched   Ⓑ fleet
  Ⓒ looming   Ⓓ cozy

4. When the sun went down, we _____ we would not be home before dark.
  Ⓐ launched   Ⓑ drifted
  Ⓒ realized   Ⓓ looming

5. The new ship was _____ at the celebration.
  Ⓐ realized   Ⓑ drifted
  Ⓒ cozy   Ⓓ launched

6. A big cat was _____ over the mouse.
  Ⓐ drifted   Ⓑ looming
  Ⓒ realized   Ⓓ fleet

Practice Book
Banner Days

Grade 2-2

Comprehension

7. This story is most like a fantasy because the story _____ .

   Ⓐ could not happen in the real world

   Ⓑ happened a long time ago

   Ⓒ has no author

   Ⓓ does not teach a lesson

8. In this story, <u>coming down in buckets</u> means _____ .

   Ⓐ pails are falling from the sky

   Ⓑ it is raining very hard

   Ⓒ the buckets are full of water

   Ⓓ the animals all fell into a bucket

9. Montigue leaves his first home because _____ .

   Ⓐ it is too cold   Ⓑ the sea floods it

   Ⓒ he is very lonely   Ⓓ the rain floods it

10. Montigue is tired when he finds a bottle to sleep in because he _____ .

   Ⓐ has been walking for days

   Ⓑ has moved his belongings into his new home

   Ⓒ has been swimming for a very long time

   Ⓓ has been visiting mouse friends

11. What is the dark shadow under Montigue's bottle?

   Ⓐ an octopus   Ⓑ a passing fish

   Ⓒ a seahorse   Ⓓ a humpback whale

12. What happens first in this story?
  Ⓐ Montigue falls out of a fish's mouth.
  Ⓑ A whale throws Montigue into the air.
  Ⓒ Montigue's bottle lands on the deck of a ship.
  Ⓓ A cat chases Montigue.

13. Why do the mice think Montigue is "funny-looking"?
  Ⓐ Montigue has big ears.
  Ⓑ They don't know Montigue is a mole.
  Ⓒ Montigue is very tall for a mouse.
  Ⓓ Montigue has lost his tail at sea.

14. What are the mice most afraid of?
  Ⓐ Barnacles   Ⓑ the sailors
  Ⓒ whales   Ⓓ mousetraps

15. What happens after Montigue tells the mice about his adventures?
  Ⓐ Barnacles surprises them all.
  Ⓑ The mice elect him their leader.
  Ⓒ The mice cheer.
  Ⓓ Montigue takes a nap.

16. How do Montigue's adventures help the mice?
  Ⓐ They make a fleet and sail away.
  Ⓑ They discover a way to tie up Barnacles.
  Ⓒ They find a way to take over the ship.
  Ⓓ They break all the mousetraps.

17. "Montigue scuttled into a hole," and "the mice scurried in every direction, collecting supplies." In this story, <u>scuttled</u> and <u>scurried</u> tell about ways _____ .

Ⓐ animals move quickly

Ⓑ to sink a ship

Ⓒ sailors get around a ship

Ⓓ sailors catch fish

18. How is Montigue's home at the end of the story different from his first home?

Ⓐ It is warm in the afternoon.

Ⓑ He has lots of friendly neighbors.

Ⓒ It is cool in the evenings.

Ⓓ It is far from the sea.

19. What kind of bottle does Montigue climb into?

_____

_____

_____

_____

20. How does Montigue feel about being captain of the fleet?

_____

_____

_____

Ruth Law Thrills a Nation

Grade 2-2

Directions: For items 1–18, fill in the circle in front of the correct answer. For items 19–20, write the answer.

Vocabulary

1. A crowd of _____ watched the games.
  Ⓐ refused   Ⓑ hospitality
  Ⓒ spectators   Ⓓ heroine

2. My brother _____ to let me use his ball and bat.
  Ⓐ refused   Ⓑ spectators
  Ⓒ hospitality   Ⓓ sturdy

3. In the play, the _____ saves the relatives from harm.
  Ⓐ stood   Ⓑ refused
  Ⓒ heroine   Ⓓ looming

4. We _____ in the line a long time.
  Ⓐ spectators   Ⓑ stood
  Ⓒ refused   Ⓓ hospitality

5. Winning that long a race is a great _____ .
  Ⓐ hospitality   Ⓑ refused
  Ⓒ stood   Ⓓ feat

6. The stranger was thankful for the _____ .
  Ⓐ feat   Ⓑ stood
  Ⓒ refused   Ⓓ hospitality

Practice Book
Banner Days

Comprehension

7. What did Ruth Law try to be the first to do?

Ⓐ fly a plane without extra gas

Ⓑ fly from New York City in a bigger plane

Ⓒ fly from Chicago to New York City in one day

Ⓓ fly to Chicago before nightfall

8. Why didn't Ruth feel cold on the morning of her flight?

Ⓐ She was too excited about her flight.

Ⓑ She had slept in four suits and a skirt.

Ⓒ It was a very warm morning.

Ⓓ She had slept in a tent on a hotel roof.

9. Lake Michigan is near _____ .

Ⓐ New York City   Ⓑ Hornell, New York

Ⓒ Chicago   Ⓓ Binghamton, New York

10. What was Ruth's "baby machine" like?

Ⓐ Her plane was the biggest and newest kind.

Ⓑ Her plane was tiny and old.

Ⓒ Her plane was built for long flights.

Ⓓ Her plane was built to carry heavy loads.

11. Which word best tells what Ruth's take-off was like?

Ⓐ fast   Ⓑ rough

Ⓒ graceful   Ⓓ easy

© Harcourt

12. To prepare the plane for Ruth's flight, mechanics _____ .

Ⓐ added five gas tanks

Ⓑ removed the lights

Ⓒ attached a special roof

Ⓓ attached a special map holder

13. Why did Ruth run out of gas before she landed in Hornell?

Ⓐ The wind didn't help push her along.

Ⓑ The wind was blowing her plane sideways.

Ⓒ She flew through a bad rainstorm.

Ⓓ She hadn't known how far Hornell was.

14. Which event happened first?

Ⓐ Ruth landed near Binghamton, New York.

Ⓑ Ruth's plane came down near Hornell, New York.

Ⓒ Ruth set an American record for flying.

Ⓓ Ruth's plane arrived in New York City.

15. Why did Ruth accept the "hospitality of strangers" outside of Binghamton?

Ⓐ Her friends did not meet her.

Ⓑ She landed there because it was getting dark.

Ⓒ Her plane got caught in a tree.

Ⓓ She was hungry and tired, so she landed there.

Grade 2-2

Practice Book
Banner Days

16. When did Ruth Law make this flight?

    Ⓐ 1916   Ⓑ 1924

    Ⓒ 1935   Ⓓ 1950

17. The book tells about someone who lived _____ .

    Ⓐ ten years ago   Ⓑ in Binghamton

    Ⓒ about 90 years ago   Ⓓ in New York City

18. This book is most like a _____ .

    Ⓐ play   Ⓑ folktale

    Ⓒ fantasy   Ⓓ biography

19. Why did Ruth wear a skirt over her four suits on the way to the plane?

_____

_____

_____

_____

_____

20. How did Ruth Law fail? How did she succeed?

_____

_____

_____

_____

_____

Grade 2-2

© Harcourt

Answer Key

THEME 1	
The Day Jimmy's Boa Ate the Wash	**How I Spent My Summer Vacation**

The Day Jimmy's Boa Ate the Wash		How I Spent My Summer Vacation	
1. B	10. B	1. A	10. A
2. C	11. B	2. B	11. D
3. A	12. A	3. D	12. A
4. B	13. B	4. C	13. B
5. D	14. D	5. D	14. D
6. D	15. C	6. B	15. D
7. C	16. A	7. D	16. B
8. A	17. A	8. A	17. A
9. A	18. A	9. C	18. B

19. because she sees the boa eating her wash
20. make-believe: because a child cannot take a large boa on a class trip

19. He thinks they are friendly.
20. make-believe; accept any one: cowboys don't kidnap a child to help them with a roundup; kidnappers wouldn't have Wallace write to his aunt; cowboys wouldn't use someone that they had to teach cowboy skills

Dear Mr. Blueberry		Cool Ali	
1. A	10. B	1. B	10. A
2. D	11. A	2. C	11. A
3. C	12. B	3. D	12. C
4. A	13. D	4. C	13. B
5. A	14. C	5. B	14. D
6. D	15. A	6. D	15. A
7. A	16. D	7. C	16. C
8. D	17. A	8. A	17. D
9. D	18. C	9. C	18. B

19. Accept any two: cornflakes, bread crumbs, a sandwich
20. Accept any two: live in salt water, know where they are going and do not get lost; eat shrimplike creatures; are migratory

19. her mother saying, "Ali, soon you'll have everything covered!"
20. sad: because it washes all her drawings away

The Emperor's Egg	

The Emperor's Egg			
1. B	10. C	19. feed the chick and keep it warm	
2. D	11. A	20. He has a pouch in his throat and can make milk for the chick.	
3. A	12. C		
4. C	13. B		
5. B	14. C		
6. A	15. D		
7. C	16. C		
8. B	17. D		
9. B	18. A		

Practice Book
Banner Days

Answer Key

THEME 2	

The Pine Park Mystery

1. C	10. B
2. D	11. C
3. A	12. A
4. B	13. B
5. C	14. B
6. B	15. B
7. A	16. C
8. C	17. A
9. D	18. D

19. her mynah bird, Dynah
20. She hopes there will be another mystery to solve.

Good-bye, Curtis

1. C	10. D
2. A	11. A
3. B	12. C
4. A	13. B
5. D	14. B
6. B	15. A
7. D	16. C
8. B	17. D
9. B	18. A

19. because people have had Curtis as their mail carrier for so long
20. because he has been delivering mail to those addresses for years

Max Found Two Sticks

1. B	10. C
2. D	11. B
3. A	12. D
4. D	13. B
5. A	14. B
6. C	15. C
7. B	16. A
8. C	17. C
9. B	18. A

19. by drumming
20. thanks

Anthony Reynoso: Born to Rope

1. D	10. A
2. A	11. D
3. B	12. C
4. D	13. C
5. C	14. A
6. D	15. A
7. C	16. B
8. B	17. C
9. C	18. D

19. He runs a landscape business.
20. He is very excited about it.

Chinatown

1. C	10. A
2. A	11. B
3. B	12. C
4. A	13. C
5. D	14. C
6. B	15. B
7. C	16. B
8. B	17. C
9. C	18. D

19. The child tells Grandma to watch out for cars; he spends time with her
20. Accept any two: the park, the cobbler shop, Dai-Dai Restaurant, the herbal shop, seafood restaurant, the outdoor market

Practice Book
Banner Days

Answer Key

THEME 3	
Abuela	**Beginner's World Atlas**

Abuela

1. B	10. B
2. C	11. A
3. A	12. C
4. C	13. D
5. A	14. B
6. A	15. A
7. C	16. B
8. C	17. C
9. A	18. B

19. It reminds her of when she first came to America.
20. Rosalba imagines it.

Beginner's World Atlas

1. C	10. B
2. D	11. A
3. A	12. A
4. C	13. C
5. D	14. A
6. D	15. B
7. A	16. C
8. D	17. C
9. B	18. D

19. North America
20. Nonfiction. The book gives facts and information about how to read maps.

Dinosaurs Travel

1. C	10. B
2. A	11. A
3. A	12. A
4. B	13. B
5. C	14. D
6. A	15. D
7. C	16. A
8. D	17. B
9. B	18. C

19. You may have an adventure.
20. Accept any two: see friends and relatives, play with your toys, eat your favorite snacks, dream about where to travel next

Montigue on the High Seas

1. C	10. C
2. A	11. D
3. B	12. B
4. C	13. B
5. D	14. A
6. B	15. C
7. A	16. A
8. B	17. A
9. D	18. B

19. a lime-soda bottle
20. Montigue enjoys guiding the ships through the waves.

Ruth Law Thrills a Nation

1. C	10. B
2. A	11. B
3. C	12. B
4. B	13. A
5. D	14. B
6. D	15. B
7. C	16. A
8. D	17. C
9. C	18. D

19. At that time, a polite woman always wore a skirt.
20. Ruth did not make her journey in one day. She set a distance record.

SELECTION COMPREHENSION TESTS
Class Record Form

Teacher _____

School _____

Student Name	Theme 1					Theme 2					Theme 3				
	The Day Jimmy's Boa Ate the Wash	How I Spent My Summer Vacation	Dear Mr. Blueberry	Cool Ali	The Emperor's Egg	The Pine Park Mystery	Good-bye, Curtis	Max Found Two Sticks	Anthony Reynoso: Born to Rope	Chinatown	Abuela	Beginner's World Atlas	Dinosaurs Travel	Montigue on the High Seas	Ruth Law Thrills a Nation
	Date/Score	Date/Score	Date/Score	Date/Score	Date/Score	Date/Score	Date/Score	Date/Score	Date/Score	Date/Score	Date/Score	Date/Score	Date/Score	Date/Score	Date/Score

A65